Study Skills

A Student's Guide for Survival

Second Edition

More than 80 Wiley Self-Teaching Guides teach practical skills from accounting to astronomy, from microcomputers to math. Some titles of related interest:

Background Math for a Computer World, second edition   Ashley
Geometry and Trigonometry for Calculus   Selby
Math Shortcuts   Locke
Math Skills for the Sciences   Pearson
Practical Algebra   Selby
Punctuation   Markgraf
Quick Algebra Review   Selby
Quick Arithmetic, second edition   Carman and Carman
Quick Calculus   Kleppner and Ramsey
Quick Typing   Grossman
Spelling for Adults   Ryan
Statistics, second edition   Koosis
Study Skills: A Student's Guide for Survival, second edition   Carman and Adams
Thinking Metric, second edition   Gilbert and Gilbert
Vocabulary for Adults   Romine
Your Library: What's in It for You   Lolley

Look for these and other Self-Teaching Guides at your favorite bookstore.

Study Skills

A Student's Guide for Survival

Second Edition

Robert A. Carman
W. Royce Adams

Santa Barbara City College

A Wiley Press Book

JOHN WILEY & SONS

New York · Chichester · Brisbane · Toronto · Singapore

Publisher: Judy V. Wilson
Editor: Elizabeth G. Perry
Managing Editor: Katherine Schowalter
Composition and Makeup: Cobb/Dunlop

Library of Congress Cataloging in Publication Data

Carman, Robert A
  Study skills.

  (Wiley self-teaching guides)
  1. Study, Method of—Programmed instruction.
2. Report writing—Programmed instruction.
I. Adams, W. Royce, joint author. II. Title.
LB2395.C26   1984   371.3'02812   84-5925
ISBN 0-471-88911-3

Printed in the United States of America

84 85 10 9 8 7 6 5 4 3 2 1

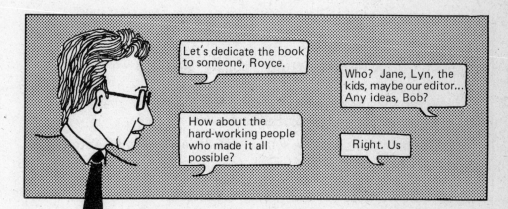

A Spelling Hint: "–seed" endings

Words that have similar endings often present spelling problems. Here is a helpful hint.

All words ending in the sound "–seed" can be divided into three kinds:

1. Only 1 word ends in –sede: supersede
2. Only 3 words end in –ceed: exceed, proceed, suceed
3. All the rest end in –cede: intercede, precede, recede, secede, . . .

Preface

Every student is engaged in a battle for survival. This battle is not simply a fight to gain intellectual food and shelter in the academic wilderness of courses and classes; rather it is for many an effort to endure. More than six out of every ten freshmen who enter American community colleges, four-year colleges, and universities never achieve their expressed academic goals. Countless more struggle through but fail to even approach their potential for success. Deficiencies in the basic learning skills—reading, writing, listening, remembering, note taking, and test taking—are at the heart of most of these failures. Yet these survival skills can be learned.

The purpose of this book is to provide assistance in learning these basic academic survival skills. The book can be used by an individual in self-study or as a text in a formal study skills course. It is organized in a programmed format that respects the uniqueness of individuals, guiding them according to their special needs and interests. Extensive testing has shown that it can be very successful in providing students with the help they need to succeed in college. We have found that the most successful users are those who accept it, not as an automatic cure for all their academic ailments, but as an opportunity, a fresh start.

Robert A. Carman
W. Royce Adams

A Tricky Quicky Quiz

A. What familiar English word is invariably pronounced wrong by every genius in the country?
B. What is the exact opposite of "not in"?
C. There are three errers in the statement of this problem. You must detect all of them to recieve full credit.

(Answers are given at the bottom of the next page.)

A. wrong
B. in
C. The first two errors are the misspellings "errers" and "re-
cieve." The third error is that there are only two errors.

Contents

Study Skills

A Student's Guide for Survival

Second Edition

CHAPTER ONE
How to Survive This Book

1————————————————

© 1972 United Feature Syndicate, Inc.

Look at that cartoon again. Read it, then go to **3**.

2————————————————

We think you're in trouble, Charlie Brown. You were told to go to **3**. Go there now.

3————————————————

This is a programmed book. In a programmed book the contents are arranged in small units called **frames.** Each frame usually requires you to respond in some way and, like Charlie Brown's book of life, the answers are *not* in the back. You answer questions on what you read and check the answers as you go along.

For example, which of the following descriptions best characterizes you? Check the one that comes closest, and then go to the frame indicated.

(a) You dig into new classes energetically but after a while you lose your enthusiasm. You start to come late, miss assignments, and skip a few classes. You get tense, waste a lot of time, and find it hard to concentrate when you have schoolwork to do. School seems to be getting tougher and tougher.

. . . go to **4**

(b) You are careful about new situations and avoid taking on more than you can handle. You try to be consistent and systematic in your studying and other schoolwork. As you progress in school you feel that you are steadily improving as a student.

. . . go to **5**

4————————————————————

We think you're in trouble, Charlie, but you've come to the right place. You *will* get help here. This book could well prove to be the "book of life" that helps you survive in the academic jungle.

You are now in Frame **4**. Notice that little number at the top left. The way to read this book is to follow *exactly* the directions you are given.

Now, go back to **3** and check answer (b).

5————————————————————

Good. That is the person we want you to become.

By now you are aware that you do not go through this book in the usual way. You travel frame to frame, sometimes forward, sometimes backward. This way, the book treats you as an individual. It recognizes that everyone has a different background of information, skills, interests, or problems. Making correct responses moves you quickly through the book. Making incorrect responses sends you to frames that provide the added information and help you need.

You will notice that material not connected to the frames appears in boxes scattered through the book. Read these at your leisure. They contain condensed practical information you may find useful.

We believe that learning should be fun and you will find that in this book we play as we work. Please never let our clowning annoy you. We have your interests at heart and are serious in our efforts to help. This book has been planned very carefully to provide the help you need. We know you're smart; you bought our book.

If you want a list of the overall objectives of this book, go to **6**; otherwise go to **7**.

6————————————————

When you finish this book, you will:

- Improve your ability to get more from classroom lectures by learning more effective ways to **listen**, **take notes**, and **remember**.
- Improve your **general reading ability** by adopting systematic procedures for reading.
- Improve your ability to read, understand, and remember **textbook reading** assignments by using the **SQ3R method**.
- Improve your ability to **write** more effective short **essays and term papers**.
- Improve your ability to score higher on both objective and subjective **examinations**.

Are you ready to go to work? If so, go to **8**.
If not, go to **7** for a pep talk.

This is a box.
Boxes, like people, come in all sizes.
Like some of our friends, this one is small, almost empty, and completely useless.

7————————————————

In most classes you will appear to your instructor as the sum of what you do in class, how you perform on exams, and what you write. What you have been in the past need have no bearing on what you can be. The fact that you are here means that you believe that you can be a better student. We believe you can too, and we have written this book to help you get there.

In the competitive grading system used in most colleges, someone loses and someone wins. Research shows that most students have never learned a systematic approach to study skills. But in college it is taken for granted that you have these skills, that you can read, write, listen, take notes, and work on exams effectively. Losers bumble through these activities. **Winners have a system**. This book will teach you to be a winner.

Ready to go to work? Go to **8**.

8————————————————

The chapters of this book have been arranged in an order that seems most useful for most students. However, you may have a pressing survival problem in one of your classes which needs immediate attention. The chapters can be read in any order.

Choose one:

- Go to the Contents for the book, select your pressing problem area, and go to the chapter and frame indicated.
- Go to Chapter 2, Frame **1**, and begin working through the book.

CHAPTER TWO
Making It in the System

GOALS AND OBJECTIVES

General Goals   When you complete this unit, you will:

1. Have increased confidence and ability in class and a better attitude toward classroom learning
2. Be better able to use the classroom situation as a part of learning
3. Be more effective at listening and note taking in class
4. Understand the importance of organizing your classroom notes and reviewing them

Specific Objectives   When you complete this unit, you will:

1. Adopt an organized approach to listening
2. Adopt an organized approach to note taking
3. Review classroom notes more often and more effectively
4. Outline and organize your classroom notes
5. Use memory aids when they are needed
6. Recognize the verbal signals used in lectures
7. Attempt to read outside assignments before they are discussed in class

MAKING IT IN THE SYSTEM

"Maybe I'll try again. The first day it was interesting, you know. I mean I really dug it. He talked about how it would be, and I really wanted to do it. But he was hard to follow in class, and it got to be a drag. I couldn't remember all that stuff . . . missed a few days, blew a test, and then things got bad at home, so I cut out."

"He was a good teacher; it just seemed like everybody else in class knew what the teacher wanted except me . . . never could figure out what he was talking about. Class was just a blur. I read most of the stuff before the tests, but still didn't do very well. Finally, when he told me I was getting a D or F, I dropped the course just before the final exam."

"I don't learn very fast and the whole thing of college is that it's set up for the guy who learns fast. . . . No, I didn't ask questions in class, he would find out how lost I was. Toward the end of the course my counselor helped a little and I got a C. If I had more time to study, it would have been a B."

Do these quotations sound familiar? They tell a story of frustration repeated daily in our colleges. Read between the lines carefully and you will see a pattern of self-defeat that appears in many students who are having trouble in college.

Students who defeat themselves

1. College is a blur for them. They are uncertain about what to do and how to do it.
2. They either don't go to counselors or teachers for help or they wait until it is too late.
3. They do not respond in class because they have learned in high school that this usually reveals that they do not understand.
4. They are busy, they work, and they have personal problems that seem never to get solved.
5. They begin the course with energy and interest, then gradually lose interest, come late, put off assignments, miss class, and finally fail or drop out.
6. They believe that if they had more time they would improve, even if they did nothing different.
7. They are tense and anxious.
8. When they settle down to study at something requiring prolonged effort, they feel tired and just do not want to do it.

A common part of the pattern is the belief that if they are interested and motivated they will learn, even if they have no learning skills. No one would expect to be able to succeed as a neurosurgeon or a pro football quarterback without training, but countless thousands of students assume they can succeed in college even if they are not skilled in reading, writing, listening, and other basic study activities. This book will help you learn those necessary skills.

Look again at that list of **eight patterns of self-defeat**. Circle those that are part of your own behavior. (We know you have problems; we all do.)

Now go to **1**.

1————————————

The best way to break out of the failure pattern is to start succeeding, and the most obviously important of all school success skills is the ability to get the most out of the time spent in class.

On what activity should you spend the most time in class? (Choose one and follow directions.)

- Reading   ☐ Go to **2**.
- Writing   ☐ Go to **3**.
- Listening   ☐ Go to **4**.
- Asking questions   ☐ Go to **5**.

2─────────────────────────────

You will have reading assignments as a part of most college classes, but class time is not usually the place to do it. During class time you can interact with your instructor, you can help him to help you. He wants that and he may be rightly upset if you read during class—even if you read your textbook.

Return to **1** and try another answer.

3─────────────────────────────

No. You will spend some time taking notes during a lecture or other class, and note taking is an important skill, but another learning skill is even more important.

Return to **1** and try again.

4─────────────────────────────

Right you are. **Listening** is a very neglected communication skill. Most students think that because they can *hear* they are listening. Allowing words to pour into your ear is not listening. We receive lots of training in reading, writing, and speaking, but no one teaches us to listen. Yet we do it all day, and it is the most used method of learning.

Research indicates that the following statements are true.

The nature of listening ⟩

- We listen in spurts. Your attention wanders so that you listen intently for 30 seconds or so, tune out for a short time, and then return. You are usually not aware that this is happening. (Did you think you had the only brain that worked that way?)
- We hear what we expect to hear. Your prejudices, past experiences, expectations, and beliefs determine what you hear. You tune out what you do not want to hear.
- We do not listen well when we are doing other things.

- We listen better when we are actively involved in the process. When you are listening to satisfy a purpose and actively searching through listening, you hear more and better.

To help you become a better listener, we have devised a set of rules called **LISAN**. The letters of this memory word stand for the key words in five rules for listening.

> **L** = **Lead**, don't follow—anticipate what's going to be said.
> **I** = **Ideas**, find them.
> **S** = **Signals**, watch for them.
> **A** = **Active**, not passive involvement.
> **N** = **Notes**, take them—organize.

Go to **6** for a detailed look at LISAN.

5―――――――――――――――――――

Not quite. Even though asking questions is important, you should not spend most of your class time doing it. Another activity must come first.
    Return to **1** and find a better answer.

6―――――――――――――――――――

The first letter in **LISAN** reminds you to **lead** rather than follow. To listen effectively in class, you must try to keep at least one jump ahead of your instructor. You **lead** rather than follow him. You try to anticipate what he is going to say next. When you guess incorrectly, try to see why you missed. This can be an exciting game. The process of leading will keep you alert, expecting to hear, and will give you a purpose.
    Leading involves two steps:

Step 1 Read outside assignments *before* you come to class. Use this reading as a preparation for listening. If you read *before* you hear the lecture, you will be more alert to important words, names, or ideas. You will anticipate them. Get to class a few minutes before it starts so you can quickly review your reading notes. This will help you to anticipate the lecture and put you in the lead at the start.

Step 2 Set up questions to keep yourself in the lead. Turn your reading and your instructor's lecture titles or opening sentences into questions. These are not questions that you ask him but ones around which you plan your listening. Make up your own questions, then listen for the answers. For example, if your history instructor announces that she will talk about "Science in the Middle Ages," you might ask:

"*What time span does 'Middle Ages' refer to?*"

"*What science did they pursue then? Chemistry? Biology? Physics?*"

"*How was science then important in people's everyday lives?*"

"*What were the important factors that helped or hindered the growth of science?*"

Other questions may become obvious as she talks. Listen. Does the instructor answer these questions?

Now, go to 7 for a little practice on this.

7——————————————————

Here are a few political science lecture titles. Make up several questions for each that might guide your listening during a lecture on the topics. An example is given for the first one.

Title	Questions
(a) Congressional reform	What kinds of reforms are needed?
(b) People in power in the United States	
(c) Political elections	

Check your answers in 9.

8 ────────────────────

Complete the following sentences.

The **L** in **LISAN** reminds you to _____ rather than follow when you are listening. Try to _____ what your instructor is going to say next.

Read outside assignments _____ you come to class.

_____ your reading notes before class.

Set up _____ to keep yourself in the lead.

Check your answers in **6**, and then go on to **10** for more on **LISAN**.

9 ────────────────────

Here are a few of the questions for listening we made up. You may have different ones that are equally useful.

(a) Congressional reform	What kinds of reforms are needed?
	What are the factors opposing reform?
	How do reforms take place?
	Who are the reformers?

(b) People in power in the United States	Who are the people in power?
	How did they get there?
	How are they related to the big corporations?
	How is their power being used?

(c) Political elections	What factors decide elections?
	What are the rules governing elections?
	What are the purposes of elections?
	Do they succeed in these purposes?

Turn to **8** for a quiz on **L = Lead**, don't follow.

10————————————————————

The **I** in **LISAN** tells you to look for the important **ideas**.

The odds are that your instructor has planned what he or she is going to say around a core of important ideas. Each lecture will introduce a few new ideas and provide explanation, examples, or other support for them. Your job is to identify the main ideas. Keep asking yourself these questions:

1. What is the point of this? What is the important new idea here? What part of what he or she is saying is support for this idea?
2. What is he or she doing? Explaining? Giving an example? Generalizing? Outlining? Showing how the idea developed? Digressing?
3. Why is he or she doing this? What is the purpose in doing it?

Your instructor will come back to the same few main ideas again and again. Be alert to them.

The following is a script of a psychology lecture. You can't hear the words, but pretend it's a lecture. Can you pick out the main ideas and supporting material?

Now I want to discuss reliability. A psychological test is said to be reliable if it gives the same results, or nearly the same results, on different occasions. The reliability of a test is measured by how consistent a person's scores are when he is retested. For example, if I use a yardstick to measure the length of this building, I would expect to get the same answer every time I measure it, to within an inch or so. The yardstick is a reliable measuring device. A psychological test's reliability is more difficult to measure because, unlike buildings, people change. They may learn from the test and change between testings.

Write the main idea being stated about psychological tests here.

———————————————————————————————————

———————————————————————————————————

Check your answer in **11**.

11————————————————————

The main idea of the lecture is that a *psychological test is reliable if it gives the same results on different occasions.* The rest of the lecture restates that idea, gives an example, and tells why reliability is difficult to measure for psychological tests.

The second letter of **LISAN** tells you to find the important **ideas**.
Go to **12**.

12———————————————————

The **S** in **LISAN** reminds you to listen for the **signal** words.

Your instructor is not going to send up a rocket when an important new idea is stated or an example is given, but he or she will use **signals** to telegraph what is coming. Every good speaker does it, and you should expect to receive these signals. For example, the instructor may introduce an **example** with "for example" as we just did. Other common signals are often given.

Lecture signal words ⟩

- The **big ideas** may be signaled with

"There are three reasons why. . . ."	(here they come)
"First, . . . Second, . . . Third, ..."	(there they are)
"And most important. . . ."	
"A major development. . . ."	(a main idea)

- The sending of **support material** may be signaled with

"On the other hand. . . ."	"Similarly. . . ."
"On the contrary. . . ."	"In contrast. . . ."
"As an example. . . ."	"Also. . . ."
"Further. . . ."	"Furthermore. . . ."
"For example, ..."	"For instance, ..."

- A **conclusion or summary** may be signaled with

"Therefore. . . ."	"Finally. . . ."
"In conclusion. . . ."	"In summary. . . ."
"As a result. . . ."	"From this we see. . . ."

- Very **important ideas** may be signaled with

"Now this is important. . . ."
"Remember that. . . ."
"The important idea is that. . . ."
"The basic concept here is. . . ."

Signals are usually ignored by those who do not know how to lisan . . . er, listen, effectively. Expect signals and be alert when you receive them.

Now turn to **14** for a bit of practice in signal receiving.

13———————————————————

The signals you should have circled were: "three ways," "first," "for instance," "second," "third," "for example," and "basic concept here is."
Go to **15** for more on **LISAN**.

14———————————————————

Circle the signal words in the following lecture script.

> There are three ways in which the reliability of a psychological test may be measured. First, a large number of persons may be tested and then re-tested later on the same test and their scores on the test and retest compared. For instance, you might give the class an IQ test today and repeat it tomorrow. The problem here is that they will remember the test tomorrow and improve their scores. So, second, we could divide the test in half and compare scores on each half. That is a little better. Third, we could make up different forms of the test and compare them with each other for the same group of people. For example, most people have IQ scores only a few points different on alternate forms of the same IQ test. The basic concept here is that somehow two tests must be given.

Check your answer in **13**.

15———————————————————

The **A** in **LISAN** reminds you to be an **Active** listener.
Listening is not just soaking up sound. To be an effective listener, you must be **active**, not passive. You must work at it, not just wait for it to work on you. This can be done in several ways:

1. Use the **class situation** for active listening. Sit close enough so that you can see and hear the instructor, and so that you can be seen and heard. Sit in the front third of the room near the center. Be on time. Look at the instructor. Respond to him or her and what is being said. If you agree, nod. Otherwise, frown, smile, laugh at the jokes, cry a little if you must, but be active.
2. Ask **questions** for active listening. Come armed with a written list of questions from your outside reading assignments or make up questions as the lecture progresses. Listen attentively to the instructor's answers. If you hesitate to ask questions for fear of appearing stupid, then ask your instructor to **explain** important points. It is an almost foolproof way to be active. You may even need

to get him or her to explain the explanations. Most instructors are eager to dig deeper into a topic, supply examples, or show off their knowledge and wit.

Active listening is effective listening.
Now go to **16**.

16————————————

The **N** in **LISAN** reminds you to take **Notes**.

In ordinary conversation we mentally interpret, classify, and summarize what is said. In classroom learning we do this more effectively by keeping written **notes**. Note taking helps us to listen by providing a **logical organization** to what we hear. It is very difficult to listen to and remember disorganized, unrelated bits of information.

If you heard someone spell out "nd, tckl, grd, cntr, hlf bk, fl bk, qrtr bk" you would find it difficult to listen and remember. Your ear would miss the sounds and your brain would fail to hold them. But when you discover the organization behind these sounds, you will recognize them at once and remember them with no effort. They are the names of the player positions on a football team, with vowels omitted: end, tackle, guard, and so on. **Organization is the key to effective listening and remembering**. Note taking is the way you find the organization. Good note taking means finding the underlying structure of what is heard, discovering the skeleton of ideas on which the instructor has built his or her lecture.

In the next section we will look at the why and how of effective note taking.

Now turn to **17** for a little quiz to see what you have learned about **LISAN**.

17————————————

Complete this outline of **LISAN**.

L = _____
I = _____
S = _____
A = _____
N = _____

Check your answer in **4**, and then go to **18**.

18 —————————————————————

Here are a few student comments you might hear in any college hallway between classes. Can you match each with the appropriate rule from **LISAN**? Try it. We've done the first one for you.

(a) "It all sounds important to me."   _____I_____

(b) "I forgot it."   _____

(c) "I fell asleep in class again."   _____

(d) "Ask questions? Man, I don't even know what he's doing!"   _____

(e) "She goes so fast I can't write it all down."   _____

(f) "I didn't realize she was giving a summary then."   _____

(g) "It is all just a blur to me."   _____

(h) "By the time I figure out what the instructor is saying, he's off on something else."   _____

Check your answers in **19**.

19 —————————————————————

The answers are

(a) __I__   The student has failed to separate out the **main ideas** from the supporting details.

(b) __N__   Taking **notes and organizing** ideas will make it easier to remember what has been heard.

(c) __A__   He is obviously not taking an **active** part in class.

(d) __L__   He is stumbling along behind the instructor instead of trying to **anticipate and lead**.

(e) __I__   When you see the **main ideas**, you do not need to write it all down.

(f) __S__   Listen for the **signal words**.

(g) _N, I_ **Organization** through **note taking** and attention to **main ideas** will bring the blur into focus.

(h) __L__   Prepare ahead of time so that you can **lead** instead of follow.

The most important part of classroom learning is having a good attitude toward the class and the instructor. **LISAN** will only help you if you use it. To do that, you must develop a positive attitude. In every class a relationship develops between you and the instructor. It can be warm, satisfying, and productive; or it can be cold and antagonistic. You can love him, hate him, or ignore him. Whatever he is like, the relationship *you* build will be a big factor in determining your success in college.

If you want to review this section on listening, return to **4**.

If you want to practice **LISAN**, go to **P1** on page 44.

Otherwise, go to **20** to learn how to take better notes in class.

In case of fire, turn to **41**.

20———————————————————

Note taking. Why take notes in class?

Why take
notes?

1. Organized notes will help you identify the core of important ideas in the lecture.
2. A permanent record will help you to learn and remember later.
3. The lecture may contain information not available anywhere else. This will be your only chance to learn it.
4. Lecture is where you learn what your instructor thinks is important, and she makes up the exams.
5. Class assignments are usually given in the lecture.
6. The underlying organization and purpose of the lecture will become clear through note taking.

We hope we have convinced you that you should take notes. Now, go to **21** for some advice on *how* to do it.

21———————————————————

Most students do take notes in class and need no convincing that notes are important. Very few really know how to do it effectively or how to use their notes once they have them. Here are **five steps to better note taking**.

1. **Preview**. As with listening, you should lead rather than follow. Relate what the instructor is saying to your own interests and needs. Read outside assignments before class so that you know where he or she is going. Organize your listening and note taking around what you already know.
2. **Select**. Listen to everything, but be selective. Do not try to copy everything. Search for the important ideas, the core of the lecture.
3. **Question**. Question continuously whether you ask your instructor the question or not. Focus your note taking around questions.
4. **Organize**. Put your notes in a logical outline form. The most important part of note taking is trying to see the material as a whole with all its relationships and interconnected parts. Organized notes are easier to remember and provide more help when you are studying for exams.
5. **Review**. It is important that you reread and revise your notes as soon as possible after you take them.

Notice that these five steps have initials O, P, Q, R, S. That may help your memory.

Go to **22**.

22————————————————————

Write down the **five steps to better note taking**.

O = _____

P = _____

Q = _____

R = _____

S = _____

And then arrange them in the order in which they are performed.

Look back in **21** to check your answer.

Two of these steps are so important that we have prepared some special help on them.

Go to **23** to learn more about **organizing** your note taking.

23————————————————

One of the most important skills you can develop is the ability to **organize, outline**, or **classify** information logically. This skill is the basis of all analytical thinking. The following sequence of frames is designed to improve your skill at organizing information.

What is the name of this group? _____

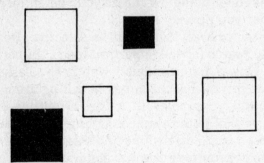

Go to **24**.

24———————————————————

This is a group of squares. Name two ways they are *different*.

1. _____

2. _____

Check your answer in **27**.

25———————————————————

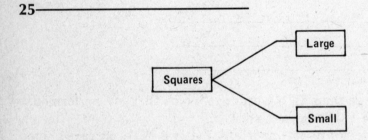

By arranging the words in this logical way, you have constructed a **concept tree**.

The set of squares shown in **23** has been divided into two groups. In one group are all the small squares and in the other group are all the large ones.

Fill in the concept tree at the top of the next page with these words:

Top,   Legs,   Table

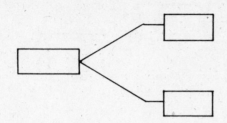

Our answer is in **26**.

NOTE-TAKING HINTS

1. Use a **shorthand notation** and abbv. wds.
2. **Use dashes** for words when the speaker goes too fast.
3. **Leave space** so that you can fill in details later.
4. **Use symbols** to call attention to important words:
   underline, CAPS, (circle), box, * , ! , ✓ , →
5. When the instructor says "this is important," get it exactly and

   * (Mark it.) ◄───

   Get a reference to the text or other source if you can.
6. **Don't erase** a mistake and don't black it out completely. Draw a single line through it. This saves time and you may discover later that you want the mistake.

26────────────────────────

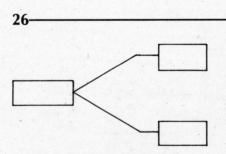

The table has two distinct parts, the top and the legs. We have made a logical arrangement of the parts of the table.

Now try these problems. Fit each set of words into a concept tree. Complete the drawing of the tree.

(a) Males
    People
    Females

(b) Book
    Cover
    Pages

(c) Land
    Ocean
    Planet
    Earth
    Air   (Draw in your own tree.)

See **29** for the correct trees.

27————————————————

1. **Size**—Large and Small
2. **Color**—Black and White

Which of these words goes in which space?

Small,   Squares,   Large

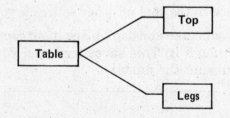

Write in the words, then check your answer in **25**.

28————————————————

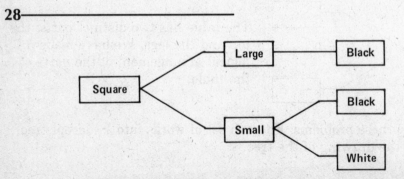

or

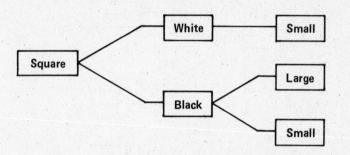

The two concept trees are equivalent. Notice that there are no large white squares.

Try this one. Sort these letters using a concept tree.

$$B \quad {}^{a} \quad {}^{b} \quad {}_{A} \quad b \quad {}^{B} \quad A$$
$${}_{A} \quad {}_{B} \quad a \quad {}_{a} \quad {}_{b}$$

First, how are they different?

1. _____

2. _____

3. _____

Look in **30** for the answer.

29——————————————————

Here are the correct concept trees.

(a)

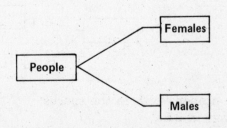

(b)

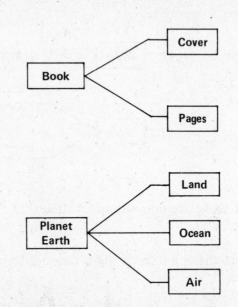

(c)

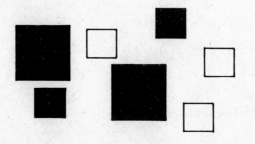

These concept trees provide logical ways of looking at the things listed. All people fall into one or the other branch of the first tree. Of course, we may have tall or short males, old or young females, and so on, producing further branches on the tree.

The group of squares

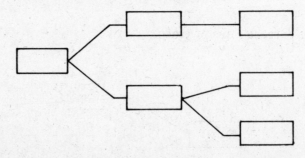

may be placed in the following concept tree.

Try it. Place the proper words in the spaces.
Check your answer in **28**.

30————————————————————

1. **Size**—large or small
2. **Shape**—capitals or lowercase
3. **Kind**—A or B

Now, make a concept tree for this set of letters.

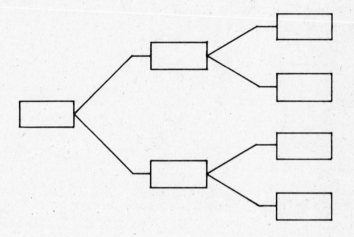

Look in **31** for the answer.

31————————————————————

Here is our tree.

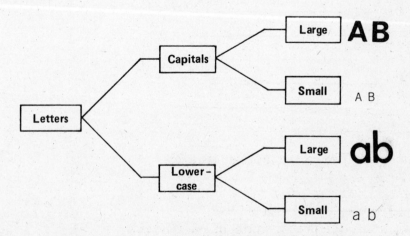

Make a concept tree for the following animals:

Eagle	Shark
Hummingbird	Guppy
Trout	Penguin
Rabbit	Mouse
Elephant	Bat

Remember:

First, see how they differ.
Next, see how they are the same.
Finally, arrange them on a tree.

Check your tree in **33**.

32──────────────────────

The outline will look like this:

   I. _____

      A. _____

          1. _____

          2. _____

      B. _____

          1. _____

          2. _____

Now try it. The correct answer is in **36**.

33──────────────────────

Kind—Birds, Fish, or Mammals
Size—Large or Small

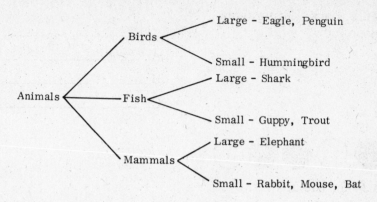

or

Kind—Flyers, Swimmers, or Runners
Size—Large or Small

In this case you put the penguin in with the rabbit and the mouse, and the bat with the hummingbird. Can you construct this tree also? Try it.

For many purposes it may be more convenient to put a concept tree into the form of an **outline**. For example, the tree

People < Females / Males   is equivalent to the outline

I. People
   A. Females
   B. Males

Write an outline equivalent to each of the following:

(a) Book < Cover / Pages

I. _____

   A. _____

   B. _____

(b) Knife, Fork, Eating tools,
    Spoon

I. _____

    A. _____

    B. _____

    C. _____

(c)

Go to **34** for the answer.

34——————————————————

(a) I. <u>Book</u>   (b) I. <u>Eating tools</u> (c) I. <u>Circles</u>
    A. <u>Cover</u>   A. <u>Knife</u>   A. <u>Black</u>
    B. <u>Pages</u>   B. <u>Fork</u>   B. <u>White</u>
                           C. <u>Spoon</u>

Now put these into outline form:

See **32** for a hint or go to **36** to check your answer.

35——————————————————

   I.   Plants
      A. Trees
          1. Pine

　　　　2. Apple
　　　　3. Oak
　　　B. Grasses
　　　　1. Wheat
　　　　2. Oats

Now return to **14** and construct a concept tree and outline for "measuring reliability of a psychological test." Draw them here.

Then go to **38** to check your answer.

36————————————————————

I. Circles _____　　　　　　　　I. Circles _____
　　A. Large _____　　　　　　　　　　A. Black _____
　　　　1. Black _____　　　　　　　　　　　1. Large _____
　　　　2. White _____　　or　　　　　　　　2. Small _____
　　B. Small _____　　　　　　　　　　B. White _____
　　　　1. Black _____　　　　　　　　　　　1. Large _____
　　　　2. White _____　　　　　　　　　　　2. Small _____

All circles in the set shown in **34** are either large or small. All large circles are either black or white. All small circles are either black or white.

Make a logical outline of the following plants:

Trees, Wheat, Pine, Apple, Grasses, Oats, Oak

Check your answer in **35**.

37———————————————

Hint:

World

I. _____

   A. _____

      1. _____

      2. _____

         a. _____

         b. _____

   B. _____

   C. _____

   D. _____

II. _____

   A. _____

   B. _____

   C. _____

   D. _____

Now try it. The answer is in **39**.

38———————————————

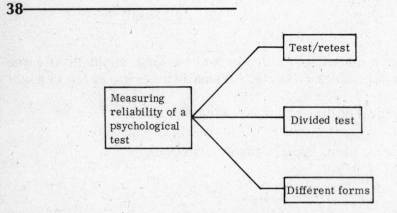

   I.   Measuring reliability of a psychological test
      A. Test and retest on the same test
      B. Divided test
      C. Different forms of a test

Here is a more difficult problem. Your geography teacher requests that you construct a logical outline of the parts of the world including:

Northern Hemisphere, North America, Africa, Australia, Southern Hemisphere, Europe, Asia, South polar regions, South America, U.S., Texas, Canada, Great Britain, Continental Europe, California, North polar regions

There is a hint in 37.
The correct answer is in 39.

There is a hint in 37.
The correct answer is in 39.

39————————————————————

World

I. Northern Hemisphere
    A. North America
        1. Canada
        2. U.S.
            a. Texas
            b. California
    B. Europe
        1. Great Britain
        2. Continental Europe
    C. Asia
    D. North polar regions

II.   Southern Hemisphere
    A. South America
    B. Africa
    C. Australia
    D. South polar regions

Notice that we use

First **Roman numerals** I, II, III . . .
Then **capital letters** A, B, C . . .
Then **ordinary numerals** 1, 2, 3 . . .
Finally **lowercase letters** a, b, c . . .

There is no special reason for this; it is simply an accepted convention. For your own notes, use anything you like but try to be consistent to avoid confusion.

Go to **40**.

40——————————————————

The **concept tree** and **logical outline** are powerful tools for thinking. By making this sort of analysis, you can discover the logic or organization behind what you are learning. Once you see the organization you will learn the material faster and remember it more completely and longer. Rather than merely memorize, you will *understand* what you are studying. Apply this tool to everything you learn. The more you use it, the better you will become at using it.

For practice, examine this book carefully and make a logical outline of its contents.

Check your answer in **42**.

41——————————————————

Not now, nosey, in case of fire!

42——————————————————

Your outline will look something like this:

  I. Title page
 II. Preface
III. How to Survive this Book
IV. Chapter I—Classroom Learning
    A. Listening
    B. Note taking
    C. Remembering
 V. Chapter II—Reading Skills
    A.
    B.
    . . . and so on.

Go to **43**.

43————————————————

Your physics instructor is lecturing on the atom, listen. (Here is a script . . . pretend.)

The simplest visual model of an atom consists of two parts: a very small, positively charged, massive core called the nucleus and a swarm of electrons moving around the nucleus. Experiments have indicated that the electrons are small, very light, and negatively charged. The nucleus itself is composed of two kinds of particles: protons and neutrons. Both are about 2000 times more massive than the electron. The proton carries a positive charge equal in size to that of the electron and the neutron is uncharged.

Make a concept tree and a logical outline of this minilecture.
If you need a hint, peek into **44**; otherwise draw your tree and outline here.

Go to **45** to check your answer when you are finished.

44────────────────────────────────

Hint:

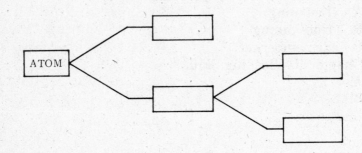

Ok? Now hustle back to **43** and get to work.

45────────────────────────────────

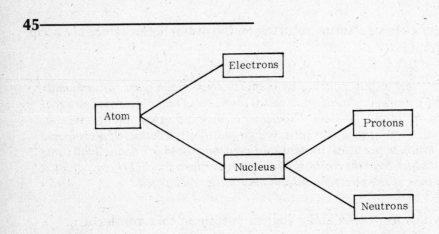

Atom
  I. Electrons
 II. Nucleus
    A.   Protons
    B.   Neutrons

Reread the script in **43**.

There are a number of descriptive terms listed—the electrons are moving, the neutrons are uncharged, and so on. Can you place these on your outline?

Try it, then turn to **46**.

46————————————————

    Atom
    I. Electron—moving, small, light, negatively charged
    II. Nucleus—small, massive, positively charged
        A.   Protons—2000 times mass of electron, positively charged
        B.   Neutrons—2000 times mass of electron, uncharged

Notice that in this way you have reduced the entire minilecture to a compact and logical form.

The logical outline is the most effective way to take notes. **Organizing**, the most important of the five steps to better note taking, means arranging the lecture information in a logical outline form so that it can be more easily understood and remembered.

The main parts of the lecture become the main, or I, II, III, . . . , branches of the tree. The key ideas in each part become the second level, or A, B, C, . . . branches. The supporting details such as descriptions, explanations, or examples are the third level, or 1, 2, 3, . . . branches. Any of the parts may be expressed as single words, phrases, or sentences. The summary, if the lecturer gives one, is a main branch of the tree. The actual symbols I, II, III, . . . , A, B, C, . . . , 1, 2, 3, . . . , may be omitted if you wish and the various levels simply indented. The important thing is that the form in which you put the notes should show the main ideas and reflect the logical organization of the lecture.

The next most important step in note taking is **reviewing**.

Go to **47** to learn more about it.

47————————————————

eviewing
otes

When an astronaut returns from a spaceflight, he is immediately "debriefed." While the flight is fresh in his memory, before any press conference or welcome takes place, and before he has had a chance to forget, he is questioned closely. He reviews all his experiences so that others involved in the space program may learn from him. Later he may review them again. Note taking requires exactly this kind of review if it is to be effective.

Review your notes **immediately** after the class—as soon as possible.

1. Are they **readable**? Clean them up. Write out abbreviations, illegible words, unfinished sentences, etc. You may not get a chance to look at them again for awhile. In a month you may not

be able to read or understand them. Make them *readable* now while they are fresh in your mind.

2. Are the notes **clear**? Add comments to make them clearer. Fill in details, add examples, restate ideas. <u>Underline</u> or otherwise

   ⌐mark⌐ important points for ★ (emphasis).

   Add a summary.

3. Are the notes **organized**? Fix up your local outline to make it better organized. No instructor is a perfect lecturer. Even the best are disorganized at times; the worst are very disorganized indeed.

Don't hand us that business about not having time to review your notes after class. You can't afford *not* to do it. Notes left unreviewed for a day are worth much less to you later. Most below-average students take disorganized notes and never review them until just before an exam. That is precisely why they are below average. You pay for not reviewing by getting a lower grade or working harder later to make up for not reviewing.

Now, go to **48**.

48————————————————

Complete these sentences by filling in the missing words. Refer to **47** if you need to.

_____ your notes _immediately_ after class.

1. Make them more _____readable_____ by writing out

   _____, rewriting _____ words,

   and finishing _____.

2. Make them _____clear_____ by adding _____,

   filling in _____, adding _____,

   or restating important ideas.

3. Make them better _____.

Check your answers in **47**. Then go to **49**.

SURVIVING IN CLASS

There are five different kinds of classes you may be attending in college. Here are some bits of advice on surviving each.

1. **Big lecture classes**. If the lecturer is disorganized, don't expect to learn much. Be sure you know what the exams will cover and what the outside assignments are. A good lecture includes an introduction where the speaker tells us what he will do, a main body where it is done, a summary where he tells what he did, and outside assignments where he tells you what to do.

2. **Small classes** or **seminars**. Here you are most visible and it is most important that you be on time, prepared, active in class, questioning. The class is usually less formally organized with more digressions and repeated points. Be selective in your note taking. Be certain you get the outside assignments—the instructor may be casual about stating them and you may not realize it is a required assignment.

3. **Individual projects**. Try to shine here. Choose projects you enjoy and already know much about. Finish on time.

4. **Lab classes**. Stay the entire time and work. Your efforts will be noticed and you can use the lab instructor as a source of help on lecture questions.

5. **Media courses**. Programmed instruction, individualized learning packages, televised lectures, computer assisted learning programs, etc. are usually a fast and efficient way to learn. Work at it as much as you must in order to learn the material.

Don't work equally hard on all courses. Work harder on the ones that are most interesting or where you have the best chance of a good grade. Two C grades can be raised to C+'s if you work equally on both, but working harder on one might get you a B in that one and a C− in the other.

49————————————————

One help in immediate review is to place your notes on a divided page. Draw a line down the middle of the page like this and **take your classroom notes on the left side**. Later when you review you will find the blank right side of the page useful for adding your own comments, questions, examples, or summaries.

During class you may want to jot notes to yourself on the right or use it to mark important ideas.

During later lectures your instructor may comment on earlier material and you may use this right-hand part for those comments.

You will find it very useful for taking notes from your outside assigned reading. You will be able to bring all your work together in this way.

The more you review your notes, the more you will use that right half of the paper.

Now go back over the above and use the right side to review what we have just said. Add your own comments and mark what you think is important.

Go to **50**.

50————————————————

For the minilecture in **43**, your split page notes might look like the following. (For some hints on how to review your notes, turn to **51**.)

Physical Science 3   Oct. 21
Structure of the atom

I. Electron . . . moving, small, light, neg. charge	Cause electric currents
II. Nucleus . . . small, heavy, pos. charge	Discovered by Rutherford . . . scattering expts.
A. Protons . . . 2000 times mass of elect., pos. charge	No electrons in nucleus ?
B. Neutrons . . . 2000 times mass of elect., no charge	How is this related to neutron bomb and radioactivity ?

51————————————————————

Later, weekly, or as often as possible during the semester or quarter, **selectively review** your notes. In this kind of review you skip quickly over what you already know and take a slow, hard look at things you do not know and should. You will find that a few minutes of selective review will help you enormously on later examinations.

Most students start out with great ambitions and good intentions. They plan to rewrite their notes into a permanent and very polished form, and to review them weekly as the course progresses. These plans generally fail because of lack of time. Keep your mind set on doing at least the minimum—**logical outlining** for organized notes and **immediate review**.

If you develop your ability to **LISAN**, and if you use *logical outlining* and *immediate review* to improve note taking, you will find that most of the material you study will drop into your memory with little special effort. But when you must memorize, there are some very effective ways to do it.

To learn how to remember better, turn to **52**.

52————————————————————

What is the title of this book? Don't look! What are the authors' names? How did we start this chapter? What was the first word in this frame? Don't peek!

Why did you forget these things? Here are a few reasons:

Why you forget > 1. You were not **interested**. You are not really interested in our names, and rightly so. You came here to learn to be a better student. Hopefully, you will remember those things that are more directly related to your personal goals. (Do you remember what the letters in LISAN stand for?)

2. You did not **select** these things to be remembered. You chose what you wanted to remember and omitted what you did not need or already knew.

3. You did not **intend** to remember. People remember what they intend to remember. Very often we cannot remember the exact appearance of the very common things we see everyday—a penny, a dollar bill, the newspaper masthead, and other familiar objects.

A good memory is a matter of wanting to remember and working at it. Here are a few rules that will help. The **first memory rule**:

1. **Focus your attention** on what you want to remember. Don't let your mind wander. Work in short, sharp spurts of concentration on one thing at a time. For example, suppose you wanted to remember the definition of a number of words for a sociology test. How would you do it?

Explain how you would do it, and then check our way in **53**.

53———————————————

Write the word to be defined on one side of a 3 × 5 file card and the definition to be remembered on the other side. Keep the pack of cards in your pocket or purse and work with them when you have a few spare moments—walking between classes, riding the bus, before class. (But not while you're driving!—especially if you are driving on the roads we drive on.)

Read the word and then try to recall the definition. Check your efforts and go on to the next card. Work for a few minutes, then put the cards back in your pocket or purse and repeat the process again later. Keep repeating it until you have the definition firmly in your head.

Go to **54** for a second memory rule.

ABBREVIATED WRITING OR ABBV. WRT.

Listen more than you write and develop a shorthand writing of your own so that you can write faster. Here are some suggested abbreviations.

lk	=	like	wrt	=	write
ex	=	example	rt	=	right
p.	=	page	i.e.	=	that is
no. or #	=	number	∃	=	there is
nos. or #s	=	numbers	→	=	means
b/c	=	because	∽	=	about (or c. for Latin
b/4	=	before			"circa," mng. "about")
wd	=	word	∴	=	therefore
ref	=	reference	etc.	=	and so on
diff	=	different	vs	=	versus, as opposed to
w/	=	with	ch	=	chapter
w/o	=	without	Q	=	question
2	=	to, two, too	lrn	=	learn

If you are in a hurry omit *a, an,* or *the,* and dot your *i*'s and cross your *t*'s later. Always use 1, 2, 3, . . . instead of *one, two, three,* . . . . Abbreviate any word by omitting the vowels.

If you try to take notes in full, you will sooner or later run into a teacher who really pours out the words. Then you will see the handwriting on the wall and it will read "Lrn to wrt lk ths b4 u go bananas."

54————————————————————

In the above example you applied a **second memory rule**:

2. **Recite.** Do something with the idea, word, or phrase you want to remember. Read it. Say it. See it. Write it. Be active with it.

Many students take notes or write out what they want to remember and then merely read the notes. To get the idea into your memory, recite actively. The more you recite, the better you will remember.

Go to **55** for another memory rule.

55————————————

A **third memory rule** is:

> 3. **Build vivid mental pictures.** Most of us are eye-minded; we remember best what we see. The more vivid the picture, the easier and longer we will remember it. Make the familiar seem strange and the strange familiar.

Suppose you had to remember that James McNeill Whistler was the artist who painted the famous portrait of a woman in a rocking chair. How would you do it? Use a vivid mental picture.

See our answer in **56**.

56————————————

Dream up a vivid, even outrageous picture. Try picturing her *kneeling* in the chair, *whistling* and *rocking*. That would be hard to forget.

Go to **57** for another memory rule.

57————————————

Another memory rule is:

> 4. **Associate the idea** to be memorized with something else. Tie it to something that sounds or looks the same. Tie it to something that is familiar and already organized. Play with it. Get your imagination into it.

For example, to remember how to spell a word or repeat a list, it is very effective to make up a sentence whose words have as their initial letters the letters of the word or list. This kind of memory aid is called **mnemonic** (say "nee-mon-ic"). "Arithmetic" becomes "A rat in Tom's house may eat Tom's ice cream." "Geography" might be "George Evans' old granny raced a pig home yesterday." Science students sometimes remember the colors of the rainbow in order from "Roy G. Biv"—red, orange, yellow, green, blue, indigo, violet. We have used mnemonic devices often in this book because they work to secure ideas in your memory.

The names of the first five books of the Old Testament are Genesis, Exodus, Leviticus, Numbers and Deuteronomy. Can you devise a mnemonic to help you remember them? Try it. Our effort is in **58**.

CLASSROOM DONT'S

Don't read in class.

Don't sleep in class—at least say "good night" if you do or you'll hurt your instructor's feelings.

Don't talk in class (except to the instructor!).

Don't sit in the back of the room.

Don't forget paper and pencil.

Don't be late.

Don't forget to hand in assignments on time.

Don't copy from other people or texts. If you borrow, give a reference.

Don't ignore any study guides, course outlines, question sets, etc. your instructor gives you. She is trying to tell you something.

Don't forget to come to class.

58—————————————————

Try "God's endless love never dies," to keep on the religious theme.

The **final memory rule** is

5. **Develop a positive attitude** toward memory tasks. Don't worry about whether you will remember something for the exam. *Expect* to remember it. Work out a memory gimmick that will assure that you do remember. Memory is not a rare gift of nature. It is a matter of wanting to remember enough to apply your mental energies and imagination to it.

Now, list the five memory rules that we have explained.

1. _____

2. _____

3. _____

4. _____

5. _____

Write out the key words, make up your own mnemonic for these five rules, and then go to **59**.

59———————————————————

THE MISSING WORDS MEMORY METHOD

Here is a memory gimmick that is especially helpful when you must memorize charts, tables, poetry, or other blocks of information.

Method	Example
Step 1 Write out a copy of the material to be memorized.	April is the cruellest month, breeding Lilacs out of the dead land, mixing Memory and desire, stirring Dull roots with spring rain.*
Step 2 First, read it. Then, attempt to recite it. Block out the words that give you the most trouble. With poetry these are usually the descriptive words.	April is the _____ month, breeding Lilacs out of the _____ land, mixing Memory and desire, stirring _____ roots with _____ rain.
Step 3 Try to visualize all the missing words, dates, numbers, and so on. Recite it until you can visualize and supply every word quickly.	
Step 4 Next, block out the next most difficult words. For poetry, these tend to be verbs. Repeat step 3 for all the blocked-out words.	April is the _____ month, _____ Lilacs _____ of the _____ land, _____ Memory and desire, _____ _____ roots with _____ rain.
Step 5 Repeat this process until all the words or numbers have been deleted and you are able to recall the material entirely.	_____ is the _____ _____, _____ _____ _____ of the _____. _____, _____ _____ and _____, _____ _____ ___ _____ with _____ _____.

This memorization technique is especially useful if you have a chalkboard handy.

*The Wasteland, T. S. Eliot, 1922.

59———————————————

1. **Focus**
2. **Recite**
3. Vivid mental **picture**
4. **Association**
5. Positive **attitude**

Our mnemonic is "<u>F</u>or <u>r</u>emembering, <u>p</u>ictures <u>a</u>re <u>a</u>dvisable."
Now, check one of the following:

- I'm a superstudent and I want
  to do some practice exercises.

  □ Good. Go to **P1**. (If you've
  already done the practice
  exercises on **LISAN**, go to
  P6, page 48.)

- I need a break.

  □ Fine. Relax awhile and return here when you're
  ready to work.

- I don't need the practice.

  □ O.K. Good luck.

Go on to Chapter 3, page 54.

THE MEMORY TRIP

When you must remember a list, such as the presidents of the
United States, the amendments to the constitution, or the seven
wonders of the ancient world, try taking a trip with the list.

1. Visualize a familiar sequence of objects or places—a walk
   around your house, your room, or your block.
2. Arrange a fixed sequence of locations and remember it—the
   dining room table, the plant by the window, and so on.
3. Take your list and associate a vivid, outlandish picture connect-
   ing each item on the list with a location. For example, to associate the amendments to the constitution with the above sequence
   of locations, you might visualize this:

First Amendment
Freedom of speech

George Washington standing
knee deep in dishes in the
kitchen sink making a speech.

Second Amendment Right to keep and bear arms	A *bear* sitting in the pantry holding a stack of peanut butter sandwiches in his arms.
Third Amendment Right to quarter soldiers	A revolutionary war soldier camped out under the dining room table hugging his piggy bank full of quarters.
Fourth Amendment Right of search	Sherlock Holmes peering at the plant by the window.

4. When you want to recall the list, **take a memory trip.** Visualize the sink and sure enough there is good old George up to his knees in suds making a *speech*. If you want the fourth amendment just race through the trip, stop at the fourth location, and Holmes will be at the ivy, magnifying glass in hand, searching.

Some amazing feats of memory can be done when you have set up a sequence of locations you know very well and when you learn to let your imagination run wild.

Chapter Two Practice Exercises

P1——————————————————

What does **LISAN** mean?

L = _____

I = _____

S = _____

A = _____

N = _____

Check your answer in **P5**.

P2————————————————————

Topics	Questions
1. The geography of Iceland	(a) How's the weather up there?
	(b) What is its most distinctive feature?
	(c) Where is it?
	(d) What are the big factors determining its weather?
2. The poetry of Victor Hugo	(a) What kind of poetry did he write?
	(b) What other poet that I know did he resemble?
	(c) What factors in Hugo's life and times influenced his poetry the most?
3. The political structure of Ancient Egypt	(a) What period of time is to be discussed?
	(b) What government structure did they have?
	(c) What factors determined the political structure?
	(d) How was it different from before or after this time?
4. Physical fitness	(a) How do I get in shape?
	(b) Is diet really very important?
	(c) What does jogging do to your heart?
5. The solar system	(a) What things are part of the solar system?
	(b) How did it come to be?
	(c) Are the stars part of it?
	(d) How is a star different from a planet?
	(e) Is there life on Mars?

Go to **P3**.

P3 ───────────────────────────────

Here are a few student comments. Can you match up the comments with the **LISAN** rule they illustrate or ignore?

L = *Lead,* don't follow
I = *Ideas*—important ideas
S = *Signal* words
A = *Active,* not passive
N = *Notes*—organize

1. "The whole lecture was based on one new idea."   _____

2. "I never read that story so I didn't know who Daisey Baker was."   _____

3. "Maybe she did say it was important, but I didn't hear it."   _____

4. "I thought that story she told was part of the book."   _____

5. "What assignment?!!"   _____

6. "Asking questions means you look bad."   _____

7. "The last time I asked a question, he told me he had just finished explaining that."   _____

8. "The whole lecture is just Chapter 3 in the text, and the book does it better."   _____

Answers are in **P4**.

P4 ───────────────────────────────

1. __I__ Look for the important new ideas.

2. __L__ Read your assignment before class.

3. __S__ Listen for the signal words.

4. __S, N__ Listen for signal words and outline your notes.

5. __S__ Listen for signal words.

6. __A__ Be active in class for better learning.

7. __L,S,A__ Read your assignment first, listen for signal words, and *then* question.

8. __L__ Read ahead.

If you have read the section on note taking, you may continue in **P6**. Otherwise, go to **20**.

P5————————————————

L = **Lead**, don't follow. Anticipate the speaker.
I = **Ideas**. Find the important ideas.
S = **Signal words**. Listen for the words that signal main ideas, supporting details, examples, summaries, etc.
A = Be **Active**, not passive. Be alert and respond. Question.
N = **Notes**. Take notes to organize what you hear.

Here is a list of lecture topics. Quickly devise several questions for each that can be used to guide your classroom listening.

Topics	Questions
1. The geography of Iceland	_____ _____ _____
2. The poetry of Victor Hugo	_____ _____ _____
3. The political structure of Ancient Egypt	_____ _____ _____
4. Physical fitness	_____ _____ _____
5. The solar system	_____ _____ _____

Some possible answers are listed in **P2**.

P6————————————————

Pretend the following is a script of a science lecture. Read it as if you were in class, and take notes on a blank sheet of note paper as you read.

I want to discuss scientific notation now . . . the way you describe the physical science measurements. Every physical quantity is described by (three parts;) (first) *the magnitude or size of the measurement;* (second,) *the precision, which tells you how well you know the measurement;* (third,) *the unit of measurement.* (For example,) *we might measure the weight of this book to be about 2 pounds. The magnitude of the measurement is 2. The units are pounds. We know the precision to the nearest pound. On the moon it would weigh about one-third pound. There are* (two kinds) *of units we will use in this course, metric and English. The pound is the English unit of weight. The newton is the metric unit of weight.* (It is important) *that you know both.*

When you have finished taking notes, go to **P7**.

P7————————————————

Before we show you our notes, answer these questions.

1. Do you have a title for your notes? If not, get one.
2. Did you list any examples? Go back to **P6**, and <u>underline</u> any examples.
3. Did you take your notes on a divided sheet of paper as explained earlier? It would be best if you did.
4. Did you look for the signal words? To be certain,, go back to **P6**, and (circle) them.
5. Did you notice the digression? Go back to **P6**, and underline it with a wavy line.

Return to **P6**, and do as directed. Then go to **P8**.

P8————————————————

This is what your marked-up version of **P6** should look like:

I want to discuss scientific notation now . . . the way you describe the physical science measurements. Every physical quantity is described by three parts: first, the magnitude or size of the measurement; second, the precision, which tells you how well you know the measurement; third, the unit of measurement. For example, we might measure the weight of this book to be about two pounds. The magnitude of the measurement is two. The units are pounds. We know the precision to the nearest pound. On the moon it would weigh about one-third pound. There are two kinds of units we will use in this course, metric and English. The pound is the English unit of weight. The newton is the metric unit of weight. It is important that you know both.

Now turn to **P9** to check your notes.

P9—

Our notes look like this:

Scientific notation

I. Three parts
   A. Magnitude or size
   B. Precision—how well you
                know it
   C. Units
      1. English
      2. Metric—important
             to know
             both
II. Examples
   A. Book weighs 2 pounds
      1. Magnitude is 2
      2. Units are pounds
      3. Precision is to
         nearest pound
   B. Weight
      1. Pound is English
         unit of weight
      2. Newton is metric
         unit of weight

He may comment on this again later, and you will need the right side to add more notes.

Go to **P10**.

P10—————————————————

Devise a mnemonic that would help you remember the names of the signs of the zodiac: Aries, Taurus, Gemini, Cancer, Leo, Virgo, Libra, Scorpio, Sagittarius, Capricorn, Aquarius, and Pisces.
  Try it. Our effort is in **P13**.

P11—————————————————

Forfeit = Foolish old runners fall easily in time.
  Did you find a better one?
  Go to **P12**.

P12—————————————————

Name the five steps to better note taking.

  1. _____
  2. _____
  3. _____
  4. _____
  5. _____

  Check your answer in **P14**.

P13—————————————————

The letters are: A, T, G, C, L, V, L, S, S, C, A, P. Try "All the great constellations live very long since stars can't alter physics."
  Surely you can find a better one.
  Suppose you consistently misspell the word *forfeit*. Can you make up a memory sentence that can be used as a mnemonic?
  Our effort is in **P11**.

P14—————————————————

The **five steps to better note taking** are:

1. **Preview** Read outside assignments before class. Organize your listening and note taking around what you already know.
2. **Select** Search for the important ideas.
3. **Question** Focus your note taking around questions.
4. **Organize** Put your notes in a logical outline form.
5. **Review** Reread and revise your notes as soon as possible after you read them.

Go to **P15**.

P15

Consider the following objects: sailboat, bicycle, raft, rocketship, motorboat, automobile, oceanliner, airplane, glider, and roller skates.

What are they called as a group? _____
How are they different?

1. _____
2. _____

Check your answer in **P17**.

P16

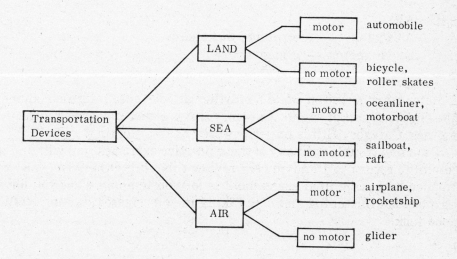

Now make a logical outline for this tree.
Check your answer in **P18**.

P17————————————————————

They are *transportation* devices.
  They differ in terms of:

1. Where they are used: land, sea, air
2. How they are run: motor or no motor

Construct a concept tree for this set of objects. You may have divided these into motor or no-motor first, but follow our division this time. Then compare your tree with ours in **P16**.

P18————————————————————

Transporation devices

  I. LAND
    A. Motor   — automobile
    B. No motor — bicycle, roller skates

  II. SEA
    A. Motor   — oceanliner, motorboat
    B. No motor — sailboat, raft

  III. AIR
    A. Motor   — airplane, rocketship
    B. No motor — glider

Motor transportation could be further divided into internal combustion engine or rocket engine. Category II.A is either inboard or outboard engines. Category II.B is either powered or free floating.

If you had trouble with any of these practice exercises, you will find it helpful to return to **1** and quickly review this unit. Otherwise, you are finished here. One final assignment is for you to apply what you have learned about listening and note taking in your classes starting NOW. Good luck.

REMEMBERING NUMBERS

Associate a specific consonant letter with each of the 10 digits.

1 = T	(1 downstroke)		6 = S	(six)	
2 = H	(2 downstrokes)		7 = L	(same shape)	
3 = N	(3 strokes)		8 = B	(same shape)	
4 = R	(R is the last letter in "four")		9 = P	(same shape)	
5 = F	(five)		0 = Z	(Zero)	

Remember these and always use the same letters.

A number such as 136 becomes TNS. Now make a word from TNS that will help you remember 136. If 136 is a weight, try *tons*. If 136 is a highway route, try *turns*. And so on. The more vivid the picture, the better. The date 1492 becomes TRPH or *trip home,* in case you need to remember Columbus' journey. The fall of the Roman Empire is often dated from 475 AD or RLF = Rome's last fling.

Try it with your phone number, social security number, driver's license number, and so on.

CHAPTER THREE
Improving General Reading Ability

GOALS AND OBJECTIVES

General Goals When you complete this unit, you will:

1. Learn to establish a reading purpose that helps you get involved in the reading assignment
2. Be able to remember better what you read
3. Be able to recognize the difference between main ideas and supporting details
4. Learn a systematic approach to vocabulary development

Specific Objectives When you complete this unit, you will:

1. Establish an identifiable purpose for every reading assignment
2. Distinguish among reading for pleasure, reading for practical application, reading for general ideas, reading to locate specific information, and reading to critically evaluate
3. Adopt a systematic approach that helps you remember what you read
4. Recognize the difference between main ideas and supporting details in reading assignments
5. Adopt a systematic approach for improving vocabulary
6. Know your average reading speed of comprehension in relation to the average college student

Place a pencil between your lips. Don't bite it with your teeth. Just hold the pencil gently with your lips. Keep it there until we tell you to take it out.

Now, with another pencil or a pen, check those items which pertain to you or which you don't understand.

☐ 1. You usually read only when you need to.
☐ 2. You generally read everything (newspapers, poems, short stories, textbooks, novels) the same way and at the same speed.
☐ 3. You generally have trouble remembering what you read.
☐ 4. You have difficulty recognizing the difference between main ideas and supporting details.
☐ 5. You generally have trouble recognizing the organization or method of presentation of an author's ideas.
☐ 6. You need to develop your vocabulary.
☐ 7. You *want* to develop your vocabulary.
☐ 8. The pencil between your lips has been moving or falling from your mouth as you have been reading this.

You may remove the pencil from your lips now. Wipe it off and continue. (If you didn't follow directions, you may have to pry it from your teeth!)

If you did not check any of the items above, skip this chapter entirely. You don't need any help.

1————————————

If you checked items 1 or 2 or both, go to **8** *now* (we'll come back to the rest of the items later); otherwise, go on to **2**.

2————————————

If you checked items 3 or 4 or both, go to **29** *now;* otherwise, go to **3**.

3————————————

If you checked item 5, go to **44** *now;* otherwise, go on to **4**.

4————————————

If you checked item 6, go to **46** now; otherwise, go on to **5**.

HOW MANY OF THESE LATIN WORD ROOTS AND AFFIXES DO YOU KNOW?

(You should know them all. If you don't, this is a good time to start learning!)

Root or Affix	Meaning	Example
ante	before	antecedent
aqua	water	aqualung
audio	hear	audio
bene	well	benefit
circum	around	circumference
corpus	body	corpse
digit	finger, toe	digital
dorm	sleep	dormitory
duc	lead, take	conductor
ex	out	exit
frater	brother	fraternity
inter	between	interstate
locus	place	locality
mit	send	transmitter
ocul	eye	oculist
pater	father	paternal
ped	foot	pedestrian
port	carry	porter
post	after	postwar
pre	before	predetermine
pro	before	project
scribe	write	transcribe
trans	across	transcontinental
video	see	video

5————————————

If you checked item 7, go to **47** now; otherwise, go on to **6**.

6————————————

If you checked item 8, go to **48** now; otherwise, go to **49**.

7————————————————————

This space is for rent.

8————————————————————

If you are here, you checked items 1 or 2, or both. Checking those particular items indicates that you probably read everything with the same approach rather than letting your **purpose for reading** guide you. For instance, when a guy receives a letter from his girl, he's going to read that letter a lot differently than he would a chapter from a chemistry book. For one thing, he's more interested in the content of the letter, right? He can relate to that letter much better than to a chapter on molecular theory. He *wants, desires, craves* to read the letter. He will probably read it several times, particularly the parts that say "I love you" or "I miss you" or "You are my Mr. Wonderful." His *purpose for reading* is to look for everything in that letter that implies all is well between him and his girl. Can you imagine this guy's mind wandering off to something else while reading his letter? Can you imagine his forgetting what the letter says? Can you imagine his failing a test on the content of the letter? Now, why isn't the desire to read a chapter on protein molecules or monetary systems or manifest destiny just as strong and meaningful?

Most teachers wish they could make their required readings as interesting as a personal love letter. But since the desire to read study material generally isn't as strong (there probably are a few people who are in love with molecules and such, but that's another story), there is often a need to create a purpose for reading that is meaningful to you. When a teacher says, "Read Chapters 5 and 6 by Friday and be ready for a quiz," the assignment itself is no purpose. Sure, your purpose for reading will be to pass the quiz and the course, but you also need a purpose that is meaningful to you—just like the guy with the love letter.

You need to establish a purpose that helps you get involved in the reading assignment.

The following frames discuss different types of purposes.

Go on to **9**.

9————————————————————

Purpose 1: Reading for Pleasure

One purpose for reading is strictly for *pleasure*. Which of the following materials do you think are read primarily with the purpose of pleasure? Check one.

1. A recipe for a cake   ☐ See **10**.
2. *People* magazine   ☐ See **11**.
3. An assigned chapter from a chemistry text   ☐ See **12**.

10————————————————

If you read recipes for pleasure, you're as unusual as the guy who reads about molecules for pleasure. Most people read recipes with the purpose of using or applying the information they read. There may be pleasure in eating the cake, but not too much in reading about it.
  Return to **9** and try another answer.

11————————————————

Right. While it's true that *People* magazine could be assigned reading for some class or other, usually the main purpose for reading material such as *People* is pleasure.
  Go on now to **13**.

12————————————————

Very doubtful. Most textbook reading is not read with pleasure as its purpose. It might turn out to be interesting or even pleasureable, but the *purpose* for reading it will not be to receive pleasure, but knowledge.
  Return to **9** and try another answer.

13————————————————

Purpose 2: Reading for Practical Application

Another purpose for reading is to *gain information which you can apply to or use in a particular situation*. Which of the following materials do you think are read primarily for the purpose of practical application? Check one.

1. A newspaper editorial   ☐ See **14**.
2. A personal love letter   ☐ See **15**.
3. A recipe in a cookbook   ☐ See **16**.

14————————————————

Probably not. A newspaper editorial is going to praise someone, take a stand on some political issue, or try to convince the reader to think a certain way. You may gain information that will help you decide how to vote on an issue, but that's not what Purpose 2 means. When you read directions in order to put a model airplane together, or you read a shop manual to learn how to run a piece of equipment, you are reading with the purpose of gaining information which you can apply or use.

Return to **13** and try another answer.

15————————————————

You're kidding! Well, maybe you're not. If the love letter says, "Yes, I'll marry you," information is being gained for practical application. However, we're discussing *purposes for reading,* and you don't read a love letter with the primary purpose of gaining usable information—not like you do a road map, the movie timetable, or TV program guides.

Return to **13** and select another answer.

16————————————————

Good choice. The purpose for reading a recipe is to use the information to actually apply it in some way. Shop manuals, laboratory manuals, dress patterns, bartender guides are all materials generally read with the purpose of practical application.

Go on to **17**.

17————————————————

Purpose 3: Reading for General Ideas

It is not always necessary to read every word on a page. If your purpose for reading is to get a general idea of the material being read, then you can read at faster speeds, skipping sections and looking only for main ideas, reading bold print headings and subheadings and summary statements usually presented at the end of the material. Just reading the questions at the end of a chapter in a textbook can give you a general idea of the content.

Which of the following materials do you think should be read primarily with the **purpose of getting a general idea of the content**?

- An encyclopedia entry on the invention
  of the compass   ☐ See **18**.
- The *Playboy* centerfold   ☐ See **19**.
- Outside reading assignments   ☐ See **20**.

18————————————————

Usually not. If you are using an encyclopedia, you are probably trying to get fairly *detailed* information, not general information.

Return to **17** and try again.

19————————————————

Hmmm. You're as strange as the guy who gets pleasure from reading about protein molecules. Most people look at the *Playboy* centerfold in great detail rather than a quick general look. Oh, well, it takes all kinds. We all have our favorite protein molecules.

Go back to **17** and try another answer.

20————————————————

That's right. It is generally impossible to read all assignments closely. Your best bet is to read supplemental or outside reading assignments more generally than you do your textbook assignments. The textbook should always be read more carefully than outside readings unless your teacher says otherwise.

Go on to **21**.

21————————————————

Purpose 4: Reading to Locate Specific Information

When you know what you are looking for, you can skim over material at very rapid rates. For instance, if your purpose is to find the definition of a word in the dictionary, or locate what time and channel your favorite program will be on TV, or find who invented the first compass or how many eggs you will need to follow the recipe you want to use, you are reading for the purpose of **locating specific information**.

Which of the following situations should involve reading primarily for the purpose of *locating specific information?*

- Relaxing with the evening newspaper   ☐ See **22**.
- Reviewing for a test   ☐ See **23**.

HOW MANY OF THESE GREEK WORD ROOTS AND AFFIXES DO YOU KNOW?

(You should know all of them. If not, now's a great time to learn them.)

Root or Affix	Meaning	Example
amphi	around, both sides	amphitheatre
anti	against	antiaircraft
auto	self	automatic
biblio	book	bibliography
bio	life	biography
dia	across, through	diameter
geo	earth	geography
graph	write, record	graphite
hetero	different, varied	heterogeneous
homo	same, equally mixed	homogenize
macro	large	macroscopic
mania	craze for	bibliomania
meter	measure	speedometer
micro	small	microscopic
mono	one	monopoly
peri	around	periscope
philo	love	philosophy
phobos	fear	phobia
phono	sound	phonograph
poly	many	polygamy
pyro	heat or fire	pyrotechnics
scope	examine	periscope
syn	together, with	synchronize
tele	far, distance	telegraph

22————————————

No. Remember, when you read for the purpose of locating specific information, you know ahead of time what you are looking for. If you can just relax with the newspaper, you will probably be looking for something interesting to read about.

Go to **23**.

23————————————————

Right. Reviewing for a test is a good example of reading to locate specific information. You will be reading to find answers to questions in the text, or questions in a study guide the instructor has given you.

Other examples of reading for specific information are locating items on maps, tables, graphs, and charts; finding things in the yellow pages; locating information in *Who's Who* or biographical dictionaries; and on and on. In other words, you do not read everything—you zero in on the specific information you need.

Go to **24**.

24————————————————

Purpose 5: Reading to Critically Evaluate

A good education should help you form your own opinions about things. When you are asked to read materials which disagree with your viewpoints, you should open your mind to what the author says and critically evaluate or judge his or her ideas against your own. You should also look for bias and propaganda on the author's part and on your part, too.

The main thing is to read with an open mind. When possible, try to read at least two different viewpoints before you make up your mind about an issue. If your education doesn't help you change your mind about some things you've always accepted as gospel truth, then you've been cheated somewhere along the line.

Which of the following situations should involve reading primarily **for the purpose of critically evaluating**?

- A magazine article claiming sexual intercourse
  causes cancer   ☐ See **25**.
- Directions for installing a dishwasher   ☐ See **26**.
- A textbook chapter on techniques for solving
  algebraic equations   ☐ See **27**.

25————————————————

You'd better believe it! An article like that ought to be read very critically.

Go on to **28**.

26————————————————

No; that type of material should be read more for Purpose 2: Reading for Practical Application. Critical evaluation can be applied to everything you read, but it is more appropriately applied to materials which deal in opinions and speculation rather than fact.

Return to **24** and try another answer.

27————————————————

More than likely, no. You'd probably read about techniques for the purpose of gaining information for application, Purpose 2. Critical evaluation should be applied most often to materials which are controversial or opinionated, such as editorials in newspapers and magazines, prepared political statements, historical articles, movie and book reviews, and other materials which deal more in opinion than fact.

Return to **24** and select another answer.

28————————————————

The five purposes which have just been presented to you were not handed down from God. There are certainly other purposes for reading. However, the differences in each purpose mentioned here should show you that before you read anything, you should ask yourself what your purpose for reading is.

Sometimes you have to create your own purpose, which may not even have been mentioned here. For instance, you don't always watch television with the same purpose. Sometimes you select a program for pleasure, sometimes because of the actors, sometimes because there is nothing better on TV, sometimes because a friend has recommended it, sometimes because an instructor has assigned it. In other words, your whole approach to watching the program will be based on your purpose for viewing it. How much you get out of the program, how involved you get in it, how much you remember about it, all depend on your purpose. The same thing applies to reading.

Now, here's a little self-check to see how well you have understood this section on purpose in reading. There are two columns on the next page. Fill in the blanks in the first column (types of reading purposes) with the letters in the other (types of reading materials).

1. ____ Reading for pleasure

2. ____ Reading for practical application

3. ____ Reading for general ideas

4. ____ Reading to locate specific information

5. ____ Reading to critically evaluate

A. This study-skills book

B. The newspaper

C. A textbook index

D. An editorial on legalizing marijuana

E. A mystery novel

Check your answers in **30**.

29————————————————

If you checked items 3 or 4 or both on the checklist, you belong here. If not, go back to **3**.

This section will deal with learning how to recognize the difference between main ideas and supporting details so that you can remember better what you read.

Here is a sample paragraph. Underline what you think is the **main idea of the paragraph**.

> There are five basic methods for developing a more powerful vocabulary. The first method is to memorize words using sight recognition by making vocabulary cards for words you want to learn. A second method is to learn phonetics so that you can sound out words you can't recognize by sight but may recognize when you hear them. Another method is to learn words by their use in context as you read. A fourth method is to learn word structure, such as the meanings of roots, prefixes, and suffixes. If none of these methods works, you can turn to a dictionary for word study.

Do your underlining, then turn to **31** to check it.

30————————————————

Compare your answers with the following:

___E___ 1. Reading for pleasure (discussed in **9**).

___A___ 2. Reading for practical application (discussed in **13**).

___B___ 3. Reading for general ideas (discussed in **17**).

___C___ 4. Reading to locate specific information (discussed in **21**).

___D___ 5. Reading to critically evaluate (discussed in **29**).

If you missed any of the above, we strongly recommend that you return to the frame indicated and re-read it.

When you feel you understand it, go to **2**.

If you got all the answers correct—fantastic! Go to **2**.

Remember that you got here by responding to statements at the beginning of this chapter.

31————————————————

You should have underlined the first sentence or at least the words *"five basic methods for developing vocabulary."*

A good way to help separate main ideas from details is to mark the passages as you read. In addition, we have circled the supporting details.

Here is how you might have marked the sample paragraph in **29**.

main idea ——— There are <u>five basic methods for developing</u> a more powerful <u>vocabulary</u>. The first method is to memorize words by (sight recognition) by making vocabulary cards for words you want to learn. A second method is to learn (phonetics) so that you can sound out words you can't recognize by sight but may recognize when you *supporting ideas* hear them. Another method is to learn words by their use in (context) as you read. A fourth method is to learn (word structure,) such as the meanings of roots, prefixes, and suffixes. If none of these methods works, you can turn to a (dictionary) for word study.

Like most (but not all) paragraphs, the **main idea** is stated in the first sentence. The sample paragraph states that there are five ways to build a vocabulary. The rest of the paragraph consists of **details** related to the main idea. The details state what the five methods are. Thus, you have the following:

Main idea: Five methods for building vocabulary
Supporting details: (a) Sight recognition
                          (b) Phonetics (sound)
                          (c) Context (use)
                          (d) Structure (word parts)
                          (e) Dictionary

If you have trouble remembering what you read, you might try taking notes as you read, notes similar to those shown above. As you study, simply stop reading occasionally and jot down the main idea and the supporting details of the passage you are reading. This physical act alone will help you.

Both note taking and marking are helpful methods for focusing your mind on what is being said. The result is that your mind can't wander to other things when you read, and you will remember better what you have read.

Now go to **32** for another exercise on this reading skill.

32——————————————

Here is another sample paragraph. Underline what you think is the main idea. Then circle the key words that show the supporting details just as the previous example shows.

1. Literal comprehension is what you use to understand and recall main ideas, to follow directions, and to follow a sequence of events. 2. Critical comprehension is what you use to distinguish fact from opinion, to evaluate and recognize bias, propaganda, and an author's inference. 3. Aesthetic comprehension is the awareness of style, humor, satire, and quality in writing. 4. Thus, there are three levels of comprehension needed for total comprehension.

- If you think the main idea is sentence 1, go to **33**.
- If you think the main idea is sentence 2, go to **34**.
- If you think the main idea is sentence 3, go to **35**.
- If you think the main idea is sentence 4, go to **36**.

33————————————————————

Sorry, wrong number. The entire paragraph is not about literal comprehension. That's only part of the paragraph's content.

Look again at the paragraph in **32** and select another answer.

34————————————————————

'Fraid not. Critical comprehension is only one type of comprehension discussed.

Return to **32** and try another answer.

SIGNAL WORDS

These words and phrases are familiar, but important for good reading because they signal what is going to happen. Learn them.

Speed-up words: These words signal that there is going to be more of the same:

also	likewise	and
more	again	more than that
moreover	furthermore	in addition

Slow-down words: These words signal that you should slow down because a change in ideas is about to occur:

but	nevertheless	rather
although	despite	however
yet	in spite of	

Here-it-comes words: These words signal that a summary or conclusion is about to be stated:

so	therefore	accordingly
thus	consequently	in summary

All these words can be guides to help you through your reading. Watch how they are used from now on. Then use them to help you read faster and better.

35————————————————————

Nope. Sentence three is a supporting detail. Try another answer.
    Return to 32.

36————————————————————

Good. You must have noticed that the last sentence is the most general
statement and mentions that there are "thus" three levels of comprehension. Sentences 1, 2, and 3 are all supporting details.
    Go to 37.

37————————————————————

Now compare your markings on the paragraph sample in 32 with the one
below:

supporting ideas   1. (Literal) comprehension is what you use to understand and
recall main ideas, to follow directions, and to follow a sequence of
events.   2. (Critical) comprehension is what you use to distinguish
fact from opinion, to evaluate and recognize bias, propaganda, and
an author's inference.   3. (Aesthetic) comprehension is the awareness of style, humor, satire, and quality in writing.   4. Thus,
main idea   there are three levels of comprehension needed for total comprehension.

    Go to 38.

38————————————————————

Pretend now that you did not mark the paragraph, but instead you were
taking notes. Fill in the blanks below with the appropriate answers.

    Main idea: _____

    Supporting details: _____

    _____

    _____

Compare your answer with ours in 40.

39————————————————————————

If you think the main idea of frames **29** to **40** is to show you the difference between main ideas and details, go to **41** now. No, don't read on; go to **41** *now!*

If you think the main idea of frames **29** to **40** is to show you how to mark a book or take notes from a book, go to **42**.

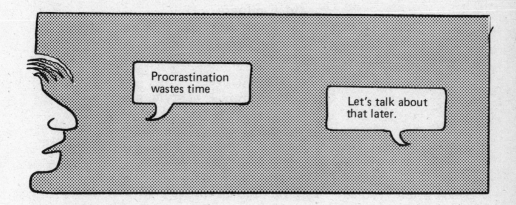

40————————————————————————

Your outline should look like this:

Main idea: Three levels of comprehension

Supporting details: 1. Literal level

2. Critical

3. Aesthetic

Notice that the main idea is a general statement. Details are more specific.

"But what if I have an instructor who wants me to know what is meant by literal, critical, and aesthetic levels of comprehension?" you ask.

That's no big deal. You just have to learn to be even more specific so that maybe your notes read like this:

Main idea: Three levels of comprehension

Supporting details: 1. Literal level
        (a) Recognize main ideas
        (b) Follow directions
        (c) Sequence of events

      2. Critical level
        (a) Fact vs. opinion
        (b) Evaluate
        (c) Recognize bias, propaganda, and
           author's inference

      3. Aesthetic level
        (a) Awareness of style, humor,
           satire
        (b) Awareness of quality

"Good grief!" you say. "Do I have to go through all that with everything I read?"

To be perfectly honest, yes and no. If you can separate main ideas from details in your mind without doing all this, the answer is no. If you have never had much experience in doing this, then yes. Practice doing this with some of your reading assignments until you can do it in your head. In time, you will find you only have to mark or take notes on certain types of materials. But reading about it here won't help one bit unless you try marking or taking notes on actual material you have to read for your course work.

Try these methods on your next assignment.

Go to **39**.

41————————————————

You're right. It may be that you don't actually need to mark or take notes from your books to recognize details from main ideas. Marking and note-taking are just useful devices to help you see the difference.

Now go back to **3**, the checklist.

42————————————————

Wrong. The main idea of those frames is to help you see the difference between **main ideas** and **supporting details**. The techniques of marking and taking notes from your book are *methods* for helping you distinguish between main ideas and details, not the main idea. In other words, one of the tasks in reading is to distinguish main ideas from supporting information. The methods of marking and note taking shown here are merely devices or ways you can learn to achieve the ability to separate details from main points.

Now go to **43** for another reading skill exercise.

43————————————————

To make certain you are on solid ground, read the following paragraph. Mark it if you want, but *read with the purpose* of distinguishing the *main idea* from *supporting details*.

Skim reading is a valuable skill to develop because of the time it can save you. Although it should never be used as a replacement for thorough reading, skimming can be used when your purpose is to read only for the main ideas or general content of a reading selection, or when you know in advance what you are looking for, such as a telephone number in a directory, a word in a dictionary, a catalog item in the library, or an index in a book. It is also a time-saving device if used properly to help you look over books placed on reserve in the library by your instructor or to cover books listed on an instructor's supplemental reading list. Wise students realize they can't read everything recommended by all their instructors. Skimming can at least help you become aware of the general content of many of those recommended books.

Now fill in the blanks below, basing your answers on the paragraph you just read.

Main idea: _____

Supporting details: _____

_____

_____

_____

_____

Complete the outline, then check your answer in **45**.

A NOTE ON SKIM READING

Businesspeople whose jobs demand that they read long, involved reports use skimming to help them finish more quickly. Students use skimming to help them with research reports, supplemental texts, and journals published in their subject areas of interest. Students can't be expected to read everything on the supplemental lists for each class they take, but they can familiarize themselves with many of them through skimming. Such familiarization offers an awareness of what is available for future reading.

Here's how to skim research reports, journal articles, and supplemental chapters:

1. **Read the first paragraph** or two at your fastest speed of comprehension to see what the general topic is about. The opening paragraphs, you will remember, usually introduce you to the author's theme or viewpoint.

2. Keep the **general theme** in mind, looking for key sentences or word phrases related to the theme. The first sentence or the last sentence is usually your best bet; but it's a good idea to let your eyes glide rapidly over the in-between lines for names, dates, or key words.

3. **Skip sections within paragraphs** that seem to contain nothing more than examples or illustrations to prove a point made in the first sentence or previous paragraphs.

4. **Look for main ideas** related to the theme of the selection. Also look for a few facts, names, or dates, to associate with the point of the article.

Don't attempt to understand or remember everything. If the material seems to be something you want to read, then slow down and read it. If it is not of interest, skip over entire sections as quickly as possible, but make certain you have at least a general idea of its contents. There are occasions, of course, when you find nothing new or nothing you need; then you skip over large selections.

44————————————————————

You shouldn't be here unless you checked item 5 on the checklist at the beginning of the chapter. It's not that there are any secrets here; it's just that you're wasting your time otherwise.

Recognizing the organization or presentation of an author's materials is discussed rather thoroughly in the section on "Reading Textbooks." So we're going to "cop out" here and just refer you to that section. If that doesn't work, you should take a good reading course under the guidance of an instructor who can give you individual help.

Go back to **4**.

45————————————————————

The main idea of the sample paragraph is that **skim reading is a useful, time-saving skill** (note the first sentence).

Supporting details:

1. Skim when looking for main ideas.
2. Skim when you know what your looking for:
   (a) Telephone numbers
   (b) Words in dictionary
   (c) Catalog items
3. Skim when you have to read reserved library books.
4. Skim when you have to read supplemental books.

If your answers were quite different from these, we suggest you try these frames again or take a reading class which will provide you with more drills than we have space for here.

If your answers were similar to these, smile at yourself in the nearest mirror and go back to **3**.

46————————————————————

You shouldn't be here unless you checked Item 6 on the checklist at the beginning of this chapter. If you didn't check Item 6, scram!

Needing to develop your vocabulary and *wanting* to do it are two different things. The point of this frame is to call your attention to the fact that your vocabulary will not increase without a *desire* and an *effort* on your part.

If you are ready to put forth that effort, go to **47** now.

If you are looking for a pill to pop that will effortlessly expand your vocabulary, forget it and go back to **6**.

UNDERSTANDING WORDS IN CONTEXT

Using **context clues** means figuring out what a word means by the way it is being used with other words in the sentence. Here are some examples:

1. *Some of his staff felt the general was being nefarious or wicked in his dealings with them.*

Notice that the word *nefarious* is actually defined within the sentence. That's why it is often a good idea not to stop reading at a word you don't know, but to read on. It may become clear what the word means through context. Of course, if you can't understand what is being said at all, then look up the troublesome words.

2. *The general was talking peace at the meeting, but was actually planning insidious military invasions.*

The little word *but* helps here. We can guess that *insidious* must mean something like sneaky, sly, or treacherous because what he was planning was the opposite of peace talks.

3. *Because his son was promoted sooner than he should have been, the general was accused of nepotism.*

It appears that the general's son might have gotten special treatment. We can infer or guess (catch that context clue?) that *nepotism* means favoritism shown to relatives.

4. *The general did not want to be accused of nepotism, so he refused to promote his son ahead of the others.*

Notice that *nepotism* is defined by showing that the general would *not* give his son special treatment.

Be alert to **context clues** that will help both your comprehension and your vocabulary development.

47————————————————————

You're in the right place if you checked Item 7 on the checklist at the beginning of this chapter. This frame is only for those readers interested in doing something about their vocabulary.

Here are four good methods for developing your vocabulary:

Method One: Take a course in vocabulary building.

Thousands of people each year buy books dealing with vocabulary building but never finish them. They start out with good intentions, but too many things "come up" that interfere with completion. If you enroll in a reading or vocabulary class, the chances are better that you will finish what you start. You are forcing yourself to schedule a portion of your time to self-improvement. Of course, people drop classes, too. But you are making a heavier commitment to yourself when you enroll in a class than you do when you just buy a book you intend to work on "when you have the time." There's only one way you'll ever have the time, and that's to make time for vocabulary improvement.

A course will also give you the chance to work in an organized way with the aid of an instructor. The instructor can help you with pronunciation and can clarify definitions of words not clearly explained in books.

Method Two: Use the vocabulary card technique.

The object of learning new words is to remember them so that you can use them in speaking and writing and to understand their meanings when you read or hear them. There are certain words which you use regularly but never think about—you just use them. When you speak with a friend, you don't analyze every word you are going to say. You have ideas, and certain familiar, overlearned words come tumbling out without thinking about them.

One of the best techniques for overlearning new words so that you can begin to use and recognize them without really thinking about them is the **vocabulary card technique**. Every day, select one word you feel is important to learn. Print that word on the front of a 3 × 5 card. Notice the example following.

```
┌─────────────────────────────────────────┐
│                                           │
│                                           │
│                                           │
│              diligent                     │
│                                           │
│                                           │
│                                           │
│            (front of card)                │
└─────────────────────────────────────────┘
```

On the back of the card, write the following information after looking up the word in the dictionary.

```
┌─────────────────────────────────────────┐
│  pronounced: dil´-a-jant                  │
│  definition:  describes steady, earnest   │
│               energetic application       │
│               and effort                  │
│  synonyms:   hard working, busy, pain-    │
│              staking, industrious         │
│  context:    Being a diligent student     │
│  she had complete notes for every lecture │
│            (back of card)                 │
└─────────────────────────────────────────┘
```

If you do this everyday, you will begin to have a growing stack of personal vocabulary cards. The trick is to spend about 5 or 10 minutes *everyday* going over and over the cards. Remember, you want to over-learn them so that you begin using them without thinking. Carry the cards around in your pocket or purse; or keep them somewhere you are sure to remember to practice them.

When you have compiled and learned about 25 or 30 cards, get some-one to check you by letting them flash the front of the card at you.

Pronounce it, give the definition, and then use it in a sentence. The best bet is to have one of your teachers check you so that you know you are pronouncing and using each word correctly.

There are boxes of vocabulary cards already printed and ready for you to learn which you can buy. However, the disadvantage is that the words used are selected by someone else and may not be the words you need or want to learn.

The boxed inserts in this book also provide you with a source of words to learn. We hope you haven't been ignoring them.

Method Three: Buy a good vocabulary textbook and use it.

It is not always easy to fit a course on reading or vocabulary building into your schedule. And you may not like the idea of making vocabulary cards, either. Here are some vocabulary books which may certainly answer your needs:

Adams, W. Royce, ed. *Mini-Course in Vocabulary Development*. Dubuque, Iowa: Educulture, Inc., 1975.

    A series of nine modules or booklets dealing with all five word attack skills, this program is usually found in Reading Labs and Learning Centers at many colleges and libraries. Tapes accompanying the booklets provide instructions and practice exercises.

Braddock, Richard. *The University Self-Teaching Dictionary Guide*. New York: Holt, Rinehart and Winston, 1979.

    Basically as the title says, this book provides you with help on how to use the dictionary to learn more words.

Brown, James I. *Programmed Vocabulary*. Englewood Cliffs, N.J.: Prentice-Hall, Inc., 1983.

    This book is another self-study program that helps you develop vocabulary through frequently appearing word roots, prefixes, and suffixes.

Davis, Nancy. *Basic Vocabulary Skills*. New York: McGraw-Hill Book Company, 1980.

    This is another programmed book dealing with roots and affixes, but it also deals with words in context and categorizes words by subject area.

Funk, Wilfred, and Norman Lewis. *30 Days to a More Powerful Vocabulary*. New York: Pocket Books, 1970.

    A day-by-day program for learning new words using all the usual vocabulary methods.

Feinstein, George W. *Programmed College Vocabulary*. Englewood Cliffs, N.J.: Prentice-Hall, Inc., 1979.

This self-help book deals with Latin and Greek derivatives and categorizes words from various subject areas such as business, law, literature and psychology.

Miriam-Webster Thesaurus. New York: Pocket Books, 1978.

This is an alphabetically arranged thesaurus of synonyms and antonyms.

There are other vocabulary books around, but these are texts you can use by yourself that do not require teacher's manuals or answer keys. You might even find some of them (or others) in your local library or bookstore.

Method Four: Read! That's right, read.

Most people with large vocabularies did not deliberately sit down and learn a big bunch of words. They gradually built a vocabulary by reading a lot. Research shows that the best method for vocabulary development is to read often and from many types of materials. Words are learned almost automatically by seeing them used in context often.

Some college students who never read much become very frustrated because their poor vocabulary keeps them from understanding textbooks. They get panicky and want a quick way to develop their word knowledge. Well, there is no quick way. It takes patience and time to develop a good vocabulary.

So start reading, friend.

Now that you are aware of some ways to develop your vocabulary, you should make some kind of commitment to yourself to do something about it. Do you trust and believe in yourself? Let's hope so; if **you** can't, who can?

Listed below are the four methods discussed. Check the one you intend to try. Just remember, a promise is a promise—even to yourself. Don't check if you don't mean it.

☐   **Method One**:   Take a course in vocabulary building.
☐   **Method Two**:   Use the vocabulary card technique.
☐   **Method Three**: Buy a book and use it.
☐   **Method Four**: Read! . . . a lot.

Now go to **6**.

WHAT'S IN A DICTIONARY?

Most people use a dictionary to check spelling or to find a word's meaning. But take a look and see what else you can learn by looking up a word in a dictionary.

Main entries show spelling and syllabication

Pronunciation

Parts of speech

Definitions

Word derivation or history

Status

Pronunciation guide

n. The treatment of disease with chemicals.

chem·ur·gy (kĕm'ər-jē, kĕ-mûr'-) *n.* The development of new industrial chemical products from organic raw materials, esp. from those of agricultural origin.

che·nille (shə-nēl') *n.* **1.** A soft, tufted cord of silk, cotton, or worsted. **2.** Fabric made of this cord. [F, "caterpillar."]

cheque. *Chiefly Brit.* Variant of check.

cher·ish (chĕr'ĭsh) *v.* To hold dear. [< OF *cher,* dear.] —**cher·ish·er** *n.*

Cher·o·kee (chĕr'ə-kē', chĕr'ə-kē') *n., pl.* **-kee** or **-kees.** **1.** A member of an Iroquoian-speaking tribe of North American Indians, formerly inhabiting SE North America. **2.** The language of this tribe.

cher·ry (chĕr'ē) *n., pl.* **-ries. 1.** A small, fleshy, rounded fruit with a hard stone. **2.** A tree bearing such fruit. **3.** The wood of such a tree. **4.** Deep or purplish red. [< VL *ceresia.*]

cher·ub (chĕr'əb) *n.* **1.** *pl.* **-ubim** (-/y/ə-bǐm'). A winged celestial being. **2.** *pl.* **-ubs.** A representation of such an angel as a winged child with a chubby, rosy face. [Heb *kərūbh.*] —**che·ru·bic** (chə-rōō'bǐk) *adj.*

Ches·a·peake Bay (chĕs'ə-pēk'). An inlet of the Atlantic Ocean, in Virginia and Maryland.

chess (chĕs) *n.* A board game for two players, each possessing an initial force of a king, a queen, two bishops, two knights, two rooks, and eight pawns, all maneuvered following individual rules of movement with the objective of checkmating the opposite king. [< OF *eschec,* check.]

chess·board (chĕs'bôrd', -bōrd') *n.* A checkerboard.

chess·man (chĕs'mǎn', -mən) *n.* A piece used in playing chess.

chest (chĕst) *n.* **1.** The part of the body between the neck and abdomen. **2.** A sturdy box with a lid, used for storage. **3.** A bureau or dresser. [< OE *cest,* box < Gmc *kistā* < L *cista.*] —**chest·ed** *adj.*

Ches·ter·field (chĕs'tər-fēld') *n.* An overcoat with a velvet collar. [< an Earl of *Chesterfield* of the 19th century.]

chest·nut (chĕs'nŭt', -nət) *n.* **1.** An edible nut enclosed in a prickly bur. **2.** A tree bearing such nuts. **3.** The wood of such a tree. **4.** Reddish brown. **5.** An old, stale joke, story, etc. [< Gk *kastenea* + NUT.] —**chest'nut** *adj.*

cheth. Variant of heth.

chev·a·lier (shĕv'ə-lîr') *n.* A member of certain orders of knighthood or merit. [< LL *caballārius,* horseman.]

chev·i·ot (shĕv'ē-ət) *n.* A heavy, twilled woolen fabric used chiefly for suits and overcoats.

chev·ron (shĕv'rən) *n.* An insignia consisting of stripes meeting at an angle, worn on the sleeve of a uniform to indicate rank or length of service.

chew (chōō) *v.* To grind (something) with the teeth. —**chew out.** *Slang.* To scold or reprimand. —**chew the rag.** *Slang.* To chat. [< OE *ceowan.* See gyeu-.] —**chew'er** *n.*

Chey·enne[1] (shī-ǎn', -ĕn') *n., pl.* **-enne** or **-ennes. 1.** A member of a tribe of Algonquian-speaking North American Indians, formerly inhabiting C Minnesota and the Dakotas. **2.** The language of this tribe.

Chey·enne[2] (shī-ǎn', -ĕn'). The capital of Wyoming. Pop. 41,000.

chi (kī) *n.* Also **khi.** The 22nd letter of the Greek alphabet, representing *kh* or *ch.*

Chiang Kai-shek (jyäng' kī'shĕk', chyäng', cháng'). Born 1887. Chinese statesman and general.

chi·a·ro·scu·ro (kē-är'ə-sk/y/ŏŏr'ō) *n., pl.* **-ros.** The technique of using light and shade in pictorial representation.

chic (shēk) *adj.* Sophisticated; elegant; modish. [< G *Schick,* skill.] —**chic** *n.* —**chic'ly** *adv.*

Chi·ca·go (shə-kä'gō, -kô'gō, -kä'gə). A city in NE Illinois, second-largest in the U.S. Pop. 3,367,000. —**Chi·ca'go·an** *n.*

chi·can·er·y (shĭ-kā'nər-ē) *n., pl.* **-ies.** Deception by trickery. [< OF *chicaner,* to quibble.]

Chi·ca·no (shĭ-kä'nō, chĭ-) *n., pl.* **-nos.** A Mexican-American. —*adj.* Of or pertaining to Mexican-Americans. [< American Span *Chicano* < Span *Mejicano,* a Mexican.]

chick (chĭk) *n.* **1.** A young bird, esp. a chicken. **2.** *Slang.* A girl; young woman.

chick·a·dee (chĭk'ə-dē') *n.* A small, gray, dark-crowned North American bird. [Imit.]

chick·en (chĭk'ən) *n.* **1.** The common domestic fowl or its young. **2.** The edible flesh of a chicken. —*adj. Slang.* Afraid. —**chicken out.** To lose one's nerve. [< OE *cicen.*]

chicken feed. *Slang.* A trifling amount of money.

chick·en-heart·ed (chĭk'ən-här'tĭd) *adj.* Cowardly; timid.

chick·en-liv·ered (chĭk'ən-lĭv'ərd) *adj.* Cowardly; timid.

chicken pox. A viral disease, usually of young children, characterized by skin eruption and slight fever.

chick·pea (chĭk'pē') *n.* The edible, pealike seed of a bushy Old World plant. [< L *cicer* + PEA.]

chick·weed (chĭk'wēd') *n.* A low, weedy plant with small white flowers.

chic·le (chĭk'əl) *n.* The coagulated milky juice of a tropical American tree, used in making chewing gum. [< Nah *chictli.*]

chic·o·ry (chĭk'ər-ē) *n.* **1.** A plant with blue, daisylike flowers and leaves used as salad. **2.** The ground, roasted root of this plant, used as a coffee admixture or substitute. [< Gk *kikhora.*]

chide (chīd) *v.* **chided** or **chid** (chĭd), **chided** or **chid** or **chidden** (chĭd'n), **chiding.** To scold; reprimand. [< OE *cīd,* strife.] —**chid'er** *n.*

chief (chēf) *n.* One who is highest in rank or authority. —*adj.* **1.** Highest in rank, authority, or office. **2.** Principal; most important. [< L *caput,* head.] —**chief'ly** *adv.*

chief·tain (chēf'tən) *n.* The leader of a clan or tribe.

chif·fon (shĭ-fŏn', shĭf'ŏn') *n.* A fabric of sheer silk or rayon. —*adj.* **1.** Of or relating to chiffon. **2.** *Cooking.* Having a light and fluffy consistency. [F, "rag."]

chig·ger (chĭg'ər) *n.* **1.** A mite that lodges on the skin and causes intense itching. **2.** Also

ă pat/ā ate/âr care/ä bar/b bib/ch chew/d deed/ĕ pet/ē be/f fit/g gag/h hat/hw what/
ĭ pit/ī pie/îr pier/j judge/k kick/l lid, fatal/m mum/n no, sudden/ng sing/ŏ pot/ō go/

48——————————————————

If you checked Item 8 at the beginning of this chapter, you are in the right place. If you didn't, go away.

The pencil wiggling and falling from your lips is an indication that you move your lips when you read silently. This is a "no-no" in reading called **vocalization**. Vocalization is fine when you are reading poetry or plays, but for normal reading, it slows you down to at least half the speed you could be reading.

While vocalization isn't as serious as lung cancer, it can be serious enough to keep you from doing your homework and other reading in much less time. What you are doing is forming the sound of every word you read and probably relying on the sound of the word rather than the sight of the word to give you meaning.

Here's a simple way to lick the vocalization problem. Stick that pencil back between your lips (*not* your teeth) and practice reading for a while. Do all your reading for the next 2 weeks with a pencil between your lips. When it falls out, put it back in. Soon the problem will disappear. All you really needed was to have your attention called to what you were doing (and a tasty pencil).

Now go on to **49**.

49——————————————————

This chapter has shown you some ways to improve your general reading ability. The real value of what you have learned depends on its use.

To prove to yourself that your time has been well spent in this chapter, pick an actual reading assignment you haven't done yet or select something you want to read from the newspaper or a magazine. Check off the following items which were covered in this section *as you read your assignment or selected material*. Do it now.

1. ☐ Establish a meaningful purpose for reading.
2. ☐ Underline the main idea in each paragraph; circle the supporting details.
3. ☐ Establish a method for learning the words you don't recognize in the material read.

When you have done it, come back to this book and go to **50**.—'bye

50——————————————————

Hi. Welcome back. How did it go?

It probably took you longer to read because you were thinking about purpose and underlining as you read. But chances are you got more from your reading and achieved better comprehension. And remember: It gets smoother and faster with practice. So keep practicing these points in all your reading. Applying the steps presented here, plus applying what you will learn in the next chapter, will make you a darn good reader.

Just remember to apply what you've learned!

Now go to **P1** for some practice sessions in general reading.

Chapter 3 Practice Exercises

P1——————————————————

Ok, here's a chance to show your stuff. Without referring back to the frames you've completed, check your talent by answering the following questions.

1. You were taught that you need to establish a purpose that helps you get involved in your reading. List the purposes discussed in this chapter.

   (a) _____

   (b) _____

   (c) _____

   (d) _____

   (e) _____

2. Give an example of 1a:

   _____

3. Give an example of 1b:

   _____

4. Give an example of 1c:

   _____

5. Give an example of 1d:

   _____

6. Give an example of 1e:

   _____

Check your answers in **P3**.

P2————————————————————

Underline what you think is the main idea of the following paragraph, and mark the key words and phrases that support the main idea.

Improving your reading ability is not easy. There are no quick-acting pills to take, no magic wand to wave over your head. The only formula for better reading is steady, conscientious practice. For instance, you should set aside a certain portion of each day to practice. Don't practice if you are tired—you need a clear and alert mind because reading involves thinking. Read from a variety of materials and apply different purposes to reading materials so that you develop a versatile reading rate.

Compare your markings with **P4**.

P3————————————————————

Your ordering may vary. That's fine. Just make sure your examples fit the right purpose.

1. a. Reading for pleasure
   b. Reading for practical application
   c. Reading for general information
   d. Reading to locate specific information
   e. Reading to critically evaluate

The following answers will vary but should be similar.

2. Reading a mystery novel
3. Cookbook, this book, a "how-to" book
4. Newspaper, magazine
5. Telephone book, dictionary, encyclopedia
6. Editorials, history textbooks, anything based on someone's opinion

Go back to **P2**.

P4————————————————————

The first sentence should be underlined. The key idea is that improving your reading is not easy. Key words and phrases which support this idea are

"No quick-acting pills"
"No magic wand"
"Steady, conscientious practice" (daily)
"Need a clear and alert mind"
"Read from a variety of materials"
"Apply different purposes"

Go on to **P5**.

P5————————————————

Underline what you think is the main idea of the following paragraph and mark the key words and phrases that support the main idea.

   A good reader tries to read more than one side of an issue and is willing to admit that his present opinions on certain subjects may be too narrow or may be wrong. The reason for reading is to broaden one's knowledge. If a reader is only going to read what he already agrees with and close his mind to opposition, he is destroying the purpose and need for education. It is very easy to read and accept those writings with which we already agree. But it is very difficult for us to read objectively writings which contain opinions we disagree with. A good reader, then, tries to read objectively from many sources.

Compare your markings with **P7**.

P6————————————————

Using the paragraph in **P5**, fill in the blanks below in your own words.

Main idea: _____

Supporting details: _____

_____

_____

_____

_____

Check your answers in **P8**.

P7————————————————

The last sentence is the key idea or topic sentence. The key words and phrases that support the topic sentence are

"Reads more than one side"
"Willing to admit opinions . . . narrow . . . wrong" (certain subjects)
"Reason for reading . . . broaden . . . knowledge"
"Close . . . mind . . . destroying . . . purpose and need for education"
"Difficult . . . to read objectively . . ."

Now go back to **P6**.

P8————————————————

Compare your answers in **P6** with these (wording may vary):

Main idea: Traits of a good reader
Supporting details: Reads objectively
Reads more than one side
Admits it when wrong
Reads to broaden knowledge
Keeps an open mind

Now go to **P9**.

P9————————————————

This frame and the next will take about 15 or 20 minutes. If you do not have that much time, do not go on. Come back here when you do. If you do have time, do not begin until you have access to a watch or a clock with a *second hand*.

You are going to time yourself while you read from the following article, "The Case for Torture." Judging from the title, state what you think the article will say about torture. ————————————

————————————————————————————————

What should be your purpose in reading this article?

_____

_____

Check your watch or clock, and write down your beginning reading time. Start exactly on the minute.

Starting time: _____

Begin reading.

THE CASE FOR TORTURE*

by Michael Levin

(1) It is generally assumed that torture is impermissible, a throwback to a more brutal age. Enlightened societies reject it outright, and regimes suspected of using it risk the wrath of the United States.

(2) I believe this attitude is unwise. There are situations in which torture is not merely permissible but morally mandatory. Moreover, these situations are moving from the realm of imagination to fact.

(3) **Death**: Suppose a terrorist has hidden an atomic bomb on Manhattan Island which will detonate at noon on July 4 unless . . . (here follow the usual demands for money and release of his friends from jail). Suppose, further, that he is caught at 10 a.m. of the fateful day, but—preferring death to failure—won't disclose where the bomb is. What do we do? If we follow due process—wait for his lawyer, arraign him— millions of people will die. If the only way to save those lives is to subject the terrorist to the most excruciating possible pain, what grounds can there be for not doing so? I suggest there are none. In any case, I ask you to face the question with an open mind.

(4) Torturing the terrorist is unconstitutional? Probably. But millions of lives surely outweigh constitutionality. Torture is barbaric? Mass murder is far more barbaric. Indeed, letting millions of innocents die in deference to one who flaunts his guilt is moral cowardice, an unwillingness to dirty one's hands. If *you* caught the terrorist, could you sleep nights knowing that millions died because you couldn't bring yourself to apply the electrodes?

(5) Once you concede that torture is justified in extreme cases, you have admitted that the decision to use torture is a matter of balancing innocent lives against the means needed to save them. You must now face more realistic cases involving more modest numbers. Someone plants a bomb on a jumbo jet. He alone can disarm it, and his demands cannot be met (or if they can, we refuse to set a precedent by yielding to his threats). Surely we can, we must, do anything to the extortionist to save the passengers. How can we tell 300, or 100, or 10 people who never asked to be put in danger, "I'm sorry, you'll have to die in agony, we just couldn't bring ourselves to . . ."

*From *Newsweek,* June 7, 1982, p. 13.

(6) Here are the results of an informal poll about a third, hypothetical, case. Suppose a terrorist group kidnapped a newborn baby from a hospital. I asked four mothers if they would approve of torturing kidnappers if that were necessary to get their own newborns back. All said yes, the most "liberal" adding that she would like to administer it herself.

(7) I am not advocating torture as punishment. Punishment is addressed to deeds irrevocably past. Rather, I am advocating torture as an acceptable measure for preventing future evils. So understood, it is far less objectionable than many extant punishments. Opponents of the death penalty, for example, are forever insisting that executing a murderer will not bring back his victim (as if the purpose of capital punishment were supposed to be resurrection, not deterrence or retribution). But torture, in the cases described, is intended not to bring anyone back but to keep innocents from being dispatched. The most powerful argument against using torture as a punishment or to secure confessions is that such practices disregard the rights of the individual. Well, if the individual is all that, important—and he is—it is correspondingly important to protect the rights of individuals threatened by terrorists. If life is so valuable that it must never be taken, the lives of the innocents must be saved even at the price of hurting the one who endangers them.

(8) Better precedents for torture are assassination and pre-emptive attack. No Allied leader would have flinched at assassinating Hitler, had that been possible. (The Allies did assassinate Heydrich.) Americans would be angered to learn that Roosevelt could have had Hitler killed in 1943—thereby shortening the war and saving millions of lives—but refused on moral grounds. Similarly, if nation A learns that nation B is about to launch an unprovoked attack, A has a right to save itself by destroying B's military capability first. In the same way, if the police can by torture save those who would otherwise die at the hands of kidnappers or terrorists, they must.

(9) **Idealism**: There is an important difference between terrorists and their victims that should mute talk of the terrorists' "rights." The terrorist's victims are at risk unintentionally, not having asked to be endangered. But the terrorist knowingly initiated his actions. Unlike his victims, he volunteered for the risks of his deed. By threatening to kill for profit or idealism, he renounces civilized standards, and he can have no complaint if civilization tries to thwart him by whatever means necessary.

(10) Just as torture is justified only to save lives (not extort confessions or recantations), it is justifiably administered only to those *known* to hold innocent lives in their hands. Ah, but how can the authorities ever be sure they have the right malefactor? Isn't there a danger of error and abuse? Won't We turn into Them?

(11) Questions like these are disingenuous in a world in which terrorists proclaim themselves and perform for television. The name of their game is public recognition. After all, you can't very well intimidate a government into releasing your freedom fighters unless you announce that it is your group that has seized its embassy. "Clear guilt" is difficult to define, but when 40 million people see a group of masked gunmen seize an airplane on the evening news, there is not much question about who the perpetrators are. There will be hard cases where the situation is murkier. Nonetheless, a line demarcating the legitimate use of torture can be drawn. Torture only the obviously guilty, and only for the sake of saving innocents, and the line between Us and Them will remain clear.

(12) There is little danger that the Western democracies will lose their way if they choose to inflict pain as one way of preserv-

ing order. Paralysis in the face of evil is the greater danger. Some day soon a terrorist will threaten tens of thousands of lives, and torture will be the only way to save them. We had better start thinking about this.

Record your finishing time: _____ Go to **P10**.

P10—————————————————————

Now subtract your starting time from your finishing time to see how many minutes and seconds it took you to read the article.

Finishing time: _____

Starting time: _____

Total Reading time: _____

Use the chart below to figure out how many words per minute you read. For instance, if you read the article in 4 minutes and 15 seconds, your rate would be 270 words per minute (WPM).

Time	WPM	Time	WPM
1:00	1090	4:00	273
1:15	872	4:15	256
1:30	727	4:30	242
1:45	623	4:45	229
2:00	545	5:00	218
2:15	484	5:15	208
2:30	416	5:30	198
2:45	396	5:45	190
3:00	363	6:00	182
3:15	335	6:15	174
3:30	311	6:30	Slow—you may want to practice increasing your reading speed.
3:45	291		

Record your WPM: _____.
Go to **P11**.

P11——————————————

Without referring back to the article, answer the following questions. If an answer is false, state why in the blanks.

T/F   1. The author believes there are times when torture should not only be permitted but demanded.

———————————————————————————

T/F   2. According to the author, torture should be the punishment of such criminals as murderers and kidnappers.

———————————————————————————

T/F   3. The author equates the barbarism of torture with mass murder.

———————————————————————————

T/F   4. The author believes in using torture only in extreme cases, such as forcing a terrorist to tell where a bomb has been planted.

———————————————————————————

T/F   5. We can probably infer, or guess, from what the author says about torture that he is also in favor of capital punishment (the death penalty) for murderers.

———————————————————————————

T/F   6. Torture in the correct circumstances, says the author, is intended to keep innocent victims from being hurt or killed.

———————————————————————————

T/F   7. The author claims that Roosevelt could have had Hitler assassinated in 1943 but refused to do so on moral grounds.

———————————————————————————

T/F   8. The author believes that a terrorist gives up his "rights" once he threatens to kill people for profit or idealism.

———————————————————————————

9. What does the author mean when he states: "Paralysis in the face of evil is the greatest danger" in reference to terrorism?

———————————————————————————

———————————————————————————

———————————————————————————

10. Why does the author believe there is little chance a wrong person would be tortured during a terrorist threat?

_____

_____

_____

Now go to **P12**.

P12————————————————

Compare your answers with these:

1. True; see paragraph 2.
2. False; see paragraph 7.
3. False; see paragraph 4.
4. True; see paragraph 5.
5. True; see paragraph 7 (the comments in parentheses).
6. True; see paragraph 7.
7. False; see paragraph 8. The author merely means that Americans would have been angered to learn that Roosevelt could have, but didn't.
8. True; see paragraph 9.
9. Being afraid to torture or act against a terrorist to preserve the lives of the innocent is worse than allowing the terrorist to get away with threats. See paragraph 12.
10. Because terrorists want public recognition; who is guilty of terrorism is not difficult to know since they usually announce themselves in their demands. See paragraph 11.

Go to **P13**.

P13————————————————

Count 10 points for each correct answer. Enter your total comprehension score here: _____ (100 points possible)

The average reader's reading rate is about 250 WPM (that's not good, just average) with about 60 to 70 points. Of course, reading rates depend upon your interest and background in the subject, your vocabulary level, and your energy level. Most people can learn to read at least twice as fast as they do before training with an increase in comprehension. You may want to consider taking a reading course that helps you develop your reading speed.

Go to **P14**.

P14———————————

Below are some questions about a special "Sports on TV" Sunday listing. Read each question and **skim** to find the answers. Do one question at a time. Try to finish in less than 30 seconds.

1. Is there a soccer game on TV Sunday morning?
   a. Yes
   b. No
2. At 10:00 a.m. who will the Pittsburgh Steelers play?
   a. Rams
   b. Patriots
   c. Browns
   d. Cardinals
3. On what channel is there a horse show?

SPORTS ON TV

Sunday

AM 9:30 (2) (12) .... NFL Today
   (4) .... NFL '80
   9:45 (34) .... Soccer
   Mexico vs. Canada.
   10:00 (2) (12) .... Pro Football
   Los Angeles Rams at New England
   Patriots.
   (4) .... Pro Football
   Cleveland Browns at Pittsburgh
   Steelers.
PM 12:00 (34) .... Round Cero
   12:45 (12) .... NFL Today
   1:00 (4) .... Pro Football

Kansas City Chiefs at San Diego
Chargers.
   (12) .... Bill Glass
   4:00 (3) (7) .... College Football '80
   (9) .... College Football
   USC vs. Washington at Los Angeles.
   4:30 (7) .... Greatest Sports Legends
   Peggy Flemming.
   8:15 (34) .... Deportes En Accion
   8:30 (Cable 2) .... Horse show
   11:30 (2) .... Sunday Sports Final
   12:30 (34) .... Round Cero

Check your answers in **P15**.

P15———————————

If you used the right clues—Soccer, Steelers, and Horse show—you should have let your eyes skim over everything that did *not* pertain to those clues. Here are the correct answers: (1) a; (2) c; (3) Cable 2. If you missed any, skim back and notice where the answers appear.

This concludes Chapter 3; but remember, every time you read, apply what you have learned here.

In Chapter 4, the next chapter, we will study how to read a textbook.

CHAPTER FOUR
Reading Textbooks

GOALS AND OBJECTIVES

General Goals   When you complete this unit, you will:

1. Believe that there is a general approach to reading textbooks that can be learned.
2. Be able to apply systematic procedures for more effective study reading.
3. Have increased confidence when reading textbook assignments.
4. Be able to score higher on exams based on textbook assignments.

Specific Objectives   When you complete this unit, you will:

1. Recall the meaning of SQ3R.
2. Adopt the SQ3R technique for study reading textbooks.
3. Attempt to survey each chapter before reading it in detail.
4. Formulate study-guide questions based on this survey before reading the chapter in detail.
5. Use some systematic method of recitation to review the content of the chapter.
6. Review the chapter after reading by referring to your notes and textbook markings.
7. Attempt to apply what has been learned by using the tear-out sheets at the end of the chapter.

If you prefer to cram for exams so that you can "get by" rather than studying for long-lasting results, go to Chapter 7.

If you want to learn an effective approach to study reading so that you can get more from your study time, read on.

Check the following if they apply to you:

☐ 1. You start reading an assignment by going to the first page of the assignment and beginning there.

☐ 2. Your mind wanders to other things while you are reading.

☐ 3. You don't pay much attention to footnotes, captions under pictures, or charts and graphs, etc.

☐ 4. You mark and underline your books as you read.

☐ 5. You panic when you take a test.

☐ 6. You spend hours studying with little to show for it.

If you checked four or more of these items, you're in the right place. If you didn't mark at least four items—well, read on for a while anyway and see if you can learn some tricks about study reading.

There it is, sitting on your desk in front of you—a $25.00 psychology textbook, heavy in weight and content. You're supposed to read an entire chapter before your 8 o'clock class tomorrow, so you turn to the assigned chapter and start reading, right?

Wrong! That would be like taking a picture without focusing on your subject and correctly setting the lens opening. What you need is a plan of attack—a plan that helps you use your study-reading time wisely and that offers you long-lasting results. Without that plan, the results of your study reading will be as fuzzy as a picture out of focus.

Although every student has his or her own approach to study reading, there are some general approaches which lead to good results. These generalities have been condensed into a very well-known and usable formula: **SQ3R**.* The term **SQ3R** is a mnemonic device (memory aid) designed to help you remember the five general steps for good study reading. *Learn these five steps in the following order:*

$$
\begin{aligned}
S &= \textbf{Survey} \\
Q &= \textbf{Question} \\
R^1 &= \textbf{Read} \\
R^2 &= \textbf{Recite} \\
R^3 &= \textbf{Review}
\end{aligned}
$$

There are many variations of this formula. But it is important that you remember each of the five steps and the proper sequence of each step. Once you learn in more detail what these steps are and how to use them, you can adapt them to fit your particular study needs. But before we get into a detailed description of the formula and how you should apply it, let's see how well you understand what you've read so far.

*Developed by Francis P. Robinson, *Effective Study*. Harper and Row, New York, 1970.

Which one of the following is correct:

- Survey, Question, Read, Review, Recite ☐ Go to **1**.
- Survey, Question, Read, Recite, Repeat ☐ Go to **2**.
- Survey, Question, Read, Recite, Review ☐ Go to **3**.

1————————————————

Nope. You probably weren't paying attention to the correct order of SQ3R, but it's important. Go back and look at the order of the formula again. Repeat it until you can recite the correct order. Then choose another answer.

2————————————————

Where did you get the idea that "Repeat" was one of the five steps? You are close but not close enough. Take another look at the formula as it was first presented. Say it to yourself until you have it. Then try another answer.

3————————————————

You're off to a good start. You remembered the right order of the formula. Now you're ready to learn each step in more detail.

Go on to **4**.

4————————————————

S = Survey

The first step toward good study reading is to **survey** or focus your attention on what you are going to read before you try to read closely. Why? Good question—glad you asked.

The reasons you should survey or preview before reading are:

1. It will **control your attention** so that your mind won't wander to other things after reading for a short time, especially if the material is boring.
2. It prepares you so that you **know what the material will be about**.

3. It awakens your subconscious to **things you may already know** about the subject being read.
4. It provides you with an **idea of the length** of the material to be read and **an idea of the time needed** to read the assignment.
5. It gives you a **purpose and direction** for reading, a purpose other than the fact the instructor assigned it. (Purpose was discussed in the previous section on reading.)

Of course, none of these things mentioned will happen if you don't survey correctly.

Before discussing how to survey correctly, check the appropriate box below and then read the designated frame:

- I am just a "get-by" student.   ☐ Go to **6**.
- I am a "super" student.   ☐ Go to **5**.

5———————————————————

If you are a super student, then you will be interested in not only how to survey an assigned chapter in a textbook but also in how to survey a book. Surveying a book consists of the following steps:

1. Read the **preface** and the **introduction**. The preface will usually tell you why the author wrote the book, what is presented in it, and for whom the book is intended. The introduction usually tells how the book should be used.
2. Read the **table of contents**. The titles of units and chapters give you a picture of the book's contents.
3. Leaf through the book noting what **visual aids** it may have, such as pictures, graphs, charts, marginal notes, subheadings, and the like. An awareness of these aids will be helpful to you when you read closely.
4. Check to see if there are reading lists of **reference works** and/or a **glossary** at the end of the book. A glossary can save you many trips to your dictionary.
5. If the chapters have **summaries**, read them quickly. Doing this may take an hour or two, but it is worth it in the long run because you will know what the book covers, what aids it offers you, and you will have a sense of direction for the course the book is being used in.

Now go get a textbook that you are using in one of your classes. No, don't sit there reading this. Go get a textbook.

Good. Now, using the following checklist, **survey** the textbook. Fill in the title and author in the blanks and then place a check mark beside each item your textbook has.

Book Title _____ Author _____

- ☐ 1. Preface
- ☐ 2. Introduction
- ☐ 3. Table of Contents
- ☐ 4. Visual aids (pictures, graphs, subheadings, comments in the margins, etc.)
- ☐ 5. Glossary
- ☐ 6. Index
- ☐ 7. Chapter summaries
- ☐ 8. Other aids not mentioned (specify what):

_____

_____

Now let's see if you really are a super student. For each of the items you checked above, read or look more carefully at what the item has to offer. When finished, write a short paragraph in the space provided which reflects what you now know about the book that you didn't know before you previewed it.

If you feel that the surveying you have just done doesn't pay off for you by the end of the semester, you can come back to this page and madly mark a big X on it.

Now go on to **6**.

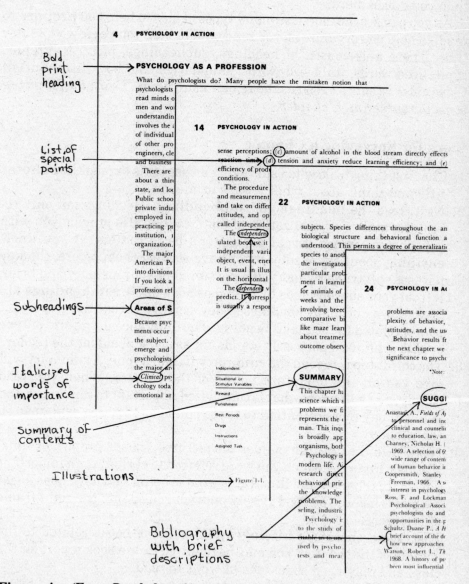

Figure A (From *Psychology for a Changing World*, by Evans and Smith, © 1970 John Wiley & Sons, Inc.)

6————————————

Taking a few minutes to **survey** a chapter before reading it closely will save time in the long run. It prepares you for what you are going to read and calls your attention to things you may already know or don't know about the material. Study carefully Figure A which shows sample pages from a typical textbook and the types of aids usually used. Do that now, then come back here.

As you can see, authors use many types of aids to help you **prepare** to read, to help you organize as you read, and to help you **review** at a later time. These aids consist of headings, subheadings, pictures, graphs, capitalized words, italicized words, summaries, and book lists. But all these aids are only as good as the reader using them. *Learn the following steps for surveying a chapter*.

Steps for Surveying a Chapter

1. The first thing to do when surveying a chapter is to read the **chapter title** and think about what it says or means.
2. Next, read the **headings** and **subheadings**. Headings not only reveal the author's organization of material but also provide you with key phrases which reveal a chapter's basic content. If you know anything about these subjects or have studied them before, the key phrases will trigger what you have stored in your memory and bring it from your subconscious to your conscious mind. **Subheadings** are breakdowns of main headings. They usually reveal the important points related to the major heading. The difference in the size of type or bold print used purposely stands out as a visual aid for the reader.
3. The third step is to read the **summary** if there is one. A summary will give you all the important points of the chapter. When you read closely, you will know what is considered important to remember and you will pay more attention to those points as they are explained in the chapter.
4. Next, read the **captions** under the pictures, charts, graphs, or illustrations. Figure A which you were referred to earlier, is an important part of this chapter and illustrates what is being said now. Looking at such aids before you read closely puts your head into the right frame of reference.
5. Last, see if there is a **bibliography** or list of books related to the content of the chapter. You may be required to do a book report for the class and may need some idea of what to read.

Now try each of the five steps for surveying on the following section of a chapter from a psychology textbook, *Introduction to Psychology: Exploration and Application*.

Emotion*

13

*From Dennis Coon, *Introduction to Psychology: Exploration and Application*, 2d ed., © 1980, West Publishing Company, St. Paul, Minn.

Voodoo Death

CHAPTER PREVIEW

In the reports of explorers and anthropologists, one finds occasional references to sudden death caused by "voodoo" or "magic." Few psychological phenomena spur more interest than these bizarre deaths. Here is an account of what happens in one tribe when a man discovers that he has been cursed by an enemy:

> He stands aghast, with his eyes staring at the treacherous pointers, and with his hands lifted as though to ward off the lethal medium, which he imagines is pouring into his body. His cheeks blanch and his eyes become glassy and the expression of his face becomes horribly distorted . . . His body begins to tremble and the muscles twist involuntarily. He sways backwards and falls to the ground, and after a short time appears to be in a swoon; but soon he writhes as if in mortal agony, and, covering his face with his hands, begins to moan . . . From this time onwards he sickens and frets, refusing to eat and keeping aloof from the daily affairs of the tribe. Unless help is forthcoming in the shape of a countercharm death is only a matter of a comparatively short time (Basedow, 1925; cited in Cannon, 1942).

This and other cases of voodoo death are difficult for those of us living in a modern society to believe. At first glance they seem to require a belief in the supernatural powers of magic. Actually, all they require is a belief in emotion. Walter Cannon (1942), a well-known physiologist, studied a large number of voodoo deaths and concluded that they really do occur.

Question: How could a voodoo curse cause death?

Cannon felt these deaths can be explained by changes in the body that accompany strong emotion. The person who has been cursed so completely believes he will die that he becomes terrified. Cannon believed the fear is so intense and lasting that it causes a heart attack or other bodily disaster.

More recent research suggests that Cannon's explanation was only partially correct. It now appears that such deaths are caused not by fear itself, but by the body's reaction to fear. After a period of strong emotion, the parasympathetic nervous system normally restores balance to the body by reversing many of the changes caused by emotion. For example, during intense fear heart rate is increased by the sympathetic nervous system; to counteract this, the parasympathetic system later slows the heart. It is now believed that the cursed person's emotional response is so intense that the parasympathetic nervous system overreacts and slows the heart to a stop (Seligman, 1974). There is more to this story (as we will see in a later section of this chapter). For now, it is enough to say that emotions are not only the "spice of life." For some, they may be the spice of death as well.

Topics Covered in this Chapter Include: parts of an emotion, theories of emotion, emotional arousal and the nervous system, sudden death, lie detectors, emotional development, expression of emotions, body language, fear, learned helplessness and depression, emotions and death, coping with depression, and the eyes as indicators of emotion.

RESOURCES

Dissecting an Emotion— How Do You Feel?

Have you ever seen a pound of anger, a quart of hate, or an ounce of joy? Of course, the question is ridiculous, yet we talk about emotions as if they were real "things." Rage, grief, ecstasy, joy, sadness, boredom—these and dozens of other terms are part of everyone's daily vocabulary. We use them so freely that it is easy to forget that emotions are *hypothetical constructs.* Like "personality," "intelligence," or "creativity," they cannot be observed directly. A person staring off into space might be bored, depressed, in love, or stoned (the last, by the way, is not an emotion). We usually must *infer* emotions from the actions and reactions of others (always a tricky business), or we must trust them to tell us how they feel. This and a number of other problems make the study of emotion difficult. The effort is worthwhile, however; emotions separate us from machines, plants, and pet rocks, and add an important dimension of meaning to human activities.

Parts of an Emotion

There are a number of facets to any emotional experience. Consider the following vivid description of emotion from Dostoevsky's *Crime and Punishment*, in which Lizavita Ivanova is about to be murdered by the main character, Raskolnikov:

> . . . When she saw him run in, she trembled like a leaf and her face twitched spasmodically; she raised her hand as if to cover her mouth, but no scream came and she backed slowly away from him toward the corner, with her eyes on him in a fixed stare, but still without a sound, as if she had no breath left with which to cry out. He flung himself forward with the axe; her lips writhed pitifully like those of a young child when it is just beginning to be frightened and stands ready to scream.

Question: What does this tell us about emotion?

Subjective Feelings   If you have ever experienced extreme fear like that described by Dostoevsky, you will recognize that **subjective feelings** are one part of any emotional experience. Emotional feelings can be classified in terms of *intensity*, *pleasantness* or *unpleasantness*, and *complexity*. For example, joy is a simple, pleasant, and intense emotion. Jealousy is a complex, unpleasant emotion that may vary in intensity. Unfortunately, it is difficult to go beyond simple classification of subjective feelings because they are extremely difficult to describe. In one rather bizarre study, women were required to crush snails between their fingers and to describe their emotional reactions. The best they could do was to *name* their emotions (Coleman, 1949). Notice that Dostoevsky did not even try to describe the feeling of fear, only the reactions.

Emotional Expressions   When a person is afraid, we observe that the hands tremble, the face contorts, and posture becomes tense and defensive. These and other **emotional expressions** are particularly important for the study of emotion in animals, and in the communication of emotion from one person to another. A marked shift in voice tone or modulation is another familiar emotional expression. This vocal change usually is accompanied by verbal expressions of emotion ranging from the nonstop abuse of rage to the surprisingly subdued last words found on flight recorders after air disasters (a common last word is "Damn," spoken calmly).

Physiological Changes   Most people closely identify a pounding heart, sweating palms, and "butterflies" in the stomach, with the experience of emotion. This observation is valid since **physiological changes** taking place in the body are the core of fear, anger, joy, and other emotions. These changes, which are the third part of an emotion, include alterations in heart rate, blood pressure, perspiration, and other bodily "stirrings." Most of these reactions are caused by release of **adrenaline** (a general bodily stimulant) into the bloodstream and by actions of the nervous system.

Question: Are physical changes in the body different for different emotions?

There are differences, but they are minor. Your heart is as likely to pound during joy as it is during anger. This is why the fourth part of an emotion is important.

Interpretation   Basic to any emotional experience is the **interpretation** placed on it. This may be seen in some interesting ways. One is by the injection of adrenaline into laboratory subjects. This typically produces "cold emotions" in which people feel "as if" they should be fearful, angry, or excited, but experience no real emotion because they know the drug caused these feelings (Marañon, 1924). A second example of the importance of emotional interpretations is provided by this case study:

> Mister J. had recently suffered a divorce, lost his job, and had assumed responsibility for two small children. Mr. J. sought the aid of a psychologist during this stressful period of his life. The psychologist reports that he would occasionally get a call from Mr. J. asking for an appointment to discuss the onset of a deep depression. More often than not, Mr. J. would call back to cancel the meeting because his feelings of depression were a "false alarm." He had misinterpreted the fatigue and other early signs of a cold or flu as feelings of depression. In the context of his life situation it is easy to see how he might be misled (Downey, 1976).

Theories of Emotion—
Four Ways to Fear a Bear

Question: What causes emotion?

There are four major theories about what takes place when a person experiences an emotion. Let's take a brief look at each.

The Commonsense Theory of Emotion   Common sense tells us that we see a bear, are frightened, and run (and sweat and yell). This explanation is far too simple to satisfy any psychologist. Besides, it is wrong. The theories of emotion that follow show why.

The James-Lange Theory (1884–1885) In the 1880s, American psychologist

William James and Danish psychologist Carl Lange proposed a different version of the relationship between emotional feelings and bodily states. James and Lange suggested that, "we are afraid of a bear because we run, or angry because we strike." In doing so, they turned the table on our usual conception of emotion. Instead of assuming that bodily changes (such as increased heart rate) *follow* a feeling such as fear, James and Lange assumed that bodily changes *precede* emotion. They argued that we see a bear, run, and *then* become conscious of fear.

To support this line of thought, James pointed out that we often do not experience an emotion until after reacting. For example, imagine that you are driving and that a car suddenly pulls out in front of you. You swerve and skid to an abrupt halt at the side of the road. Only after you have come to a stop do you notice your pounding heart, rapid breathing, and tense muscles—and recognize your fear. The James-Lange theory of emotion may help explain an interesting effect you have probably observed. When you are feeling "down" or sad, forcing yourself to smile will sometimes be followed by an actual improvement in your mood (Laird, 1974).

The Cannon-Bard Theory (1927) American physiologist Walter Cannon and his student Phillip Bard found a number of reasons to reject the James-Lange theory. While agreeing that the body becomes stirred up during emotion, Cannon and Bard noted that there are only slight differences in the physiology of various emotions. These differences are just not enough to allow for the rich and varied emotional life that humans experience. As a matter of fact, persons with spinal cord injuries still experience emotion, even though they may be unable to feel the normal sensations of bodily arousal (Hohmann, 1966).

Question: How do Cannon and Bard interpret emotion?

For the reasons just stated, and a number of others, Cannon (1932) proposed that emotional feelings and bodily arousal occur at the same time. In this version, seeing a bear activates the cortex, the thalamus, and the hypothalamus of the brain. Cannon believed the thalamus alerts both the hypothalamus and the cortex for action, but before the hypothalamus arouses the body, the cortex must give the go-ahead by deciding that the bear is dangerous. If the bear is seen as dangerous, bodily arousal, running, and feelings of fear will all be generated at the same time by brain activity.

Let's summarize: The commonsense theory of emotion is wrong. The James-Lange theory says emotion *is* bodily arousal and that the body must be aroused *before* an emotion is experienced. The Cannon-Bard theory moved emotions from the body to the head by saying that emotions are organized in the brain and that emotional feelings and bodily expressions occur simultaneously. There is a fourth possibility.

Schachter's Cognitive Theory of Emotion (1971)   The previous theories are mostly concerned with emotion as physiological response. In Stanley Schachter's view, cognitive (mental) factors are also major determinants of emotions. According to Schachter, emotion is a combination of physical arousal and the *label* that is applied to that arousal. In other words, Schachter assumes that when people become physically aroused, they have a need to interpret the arousal. The label (such as anger, fear, or happiness) applied to emotional feelings will be influenced by past experiences, the situation in which people find themselves, and the reactions of those around them.

To test this theory, Schachter and Singer (1962) injected subjects with the drug adrenaline. Subjects were misinformed about the drug they were receiving. Instead of adrenaline, they were told that they were receiving a vitamin being tested for its effects on vision. While this vitamin was supposedly taking effect, subjects were asked to wait in a room with another subject. The second "subject" was really an accomplice of the experimenters who was trained to act very *happy* or very *angry*. As the adrenaline began to take effect, subjects found themselves in a room with someone who was joking, doodling, flying paper airplanes, and generally acting extremely happy *or* with someone who was acting very angry by criticizing the experimental questionnaire, complaining about the wait, and eventually stomping out of the room.

Question: What does this have to do with the person's emotions?

Schachter and Singer were interested in what would happen when the adrenaline took effect and a subject began to feel aroused. Would the actions of the other "student" influence the emotions felt by the real subject? They found that if subjects were *correctly informed* about the effects of adrenaline (pounding heart, trembling hands), the antics of the actor had little effect on them. Informed subjects knew the drug had caused their unusual feelings. Those who were *uninformed* or *misinformed* (told that the drug would cause numbness and itching) were highly influenced by the "anger" and "happiness" conditions.*

Faced with a stirred-up body and no explanation for the way they were feeling, subjects became happy or angry in accordance with the situation in which they found themselves. Schachter would predict, then, that if you met a bear, you would be aroused. If the bear seemed unfriendly, you would interpret your arousal as fear, and if the bear was throwing paper airplanes, you would be happy, amazed, and relieved!

Further support for the cognitive theory of emotion comes from an experiment in which subjects watched a slapstick movie (Schachter and Wheeler, 1962). Before viewing the movie, one-third of the subjects received an injection of adrenaline, one-third got a placebo injection, and the remaining subjects were given a tranquilizer. Subjects who received the adrenaline rated the movie funniest and showed the most obvious amusement while watching it. Those given the tranquilizer were least amused, and the placebo group fell in between. Again the explanation would be that the adrenaline group experienced arousal that was then interpreted as amusement in the context of watching the movie. This and similar experiments make it clear that emotion is much more than just an agitated body. Perception, experience, attitudes, judgment, and many other

*To be accurate it must be noted that one recent attempt to repeat the Schachter-Singer study failed to get the same results (Marshall, 1976; Zimbardo, 1977). Remember, however, that a theory is not proved or disproved by a single experiment. A large number of other studies lend support to the cognitive theory of emotion.

more clearly "mental" factors also affect emotion.

Attribution We now move from slapstick movies and fear of bear bodies to appreciation of bare bodies. Stuart Valins (1967) has added an interesting refinement to Schachter's theory of cognitive labeling. According to Valins, perception of emotion in any situation depends on what feelings of physical arousal are attributed to. To demonstrate **attribution**, Valins (1966) showed undergraduate male students a series of slides of nude females. While watching the slides, subjects heard an amplified heartbeat that they believed was their own. In reality they were listening to a recorded heartbeat carefully designed to beat *louder* and *stronger* when some (but not all) of the slides were shown.

After viewing the slides, subjects were asked to rate which they found most attractive. Students exposed to the false heart-rate information consistently rated slides that were paired with a "pounding heart" as the most attractive. In other words, when a subject saw a slide and heard his heartbeat become more pronounced, he attributed his "emotion" to the slide and his interpretation seems to have been, "Now that one I like!"

Question: That seems somewhat artificial. Does it really make any difference what arousal is attributed to?

To further illustrate attribution, imagine yourself in this situation: You are taking (and failing) an important and extremely difficult test. The person giving the test departs for a few minutes, leaving the test answers behind. Do you give in to temptation and cheat? It may depend on how much guilt or fear you feel as you consider cheating. This is the dilemma people faced in an experiment by Dienstbier and Munter (1971). Before beginning the test, each subject took a placebo pill. Some were told to expect reactions from the pill resembling fear. Others thought the pill would cause neutral side effects unrelated to emotion.

Question: Did one group cheat more than the other?

Yes. Subjects who expected fearlike reactions from the pill cheated more than those who expected neutral side effects. The people who cheated apparently blamed the butterflies in their stomach and their pounding heart on the pill, rather than on guilt or fear. As a result they were less inhibited about cheating.

You might still be wondering how attribution works in the "real world." Consider what happens when parents interfere with the budding romance of a son or daughter. Often, trying to break up a young couple's relationship *intensifies* their feelings for one another. Parental interference adds frustration, anger, and fear or excitement (as in seeing each other "on the sly") to the couple's feelings. Since they already care for one another they are likely to attribute all this added emotion to "true love" (Walster, 1971).

Attribution theory predicts that you are most likely to "love" someone who gets you stirred up emotionally, even when fear, anger, frustration, or rejection is part of the formula. Thus, if you want to successfully propose to someone, take them out to the middle of a narrow, windswept suspension bridge over a deep chasm and look them in the eyes. As their heart pounds wildly (from being on the bridge, not from your irresistible charms), tell them you love them. Attribution theory predicts they will conclude, "Oh wow, I must love you too!"

LEARNING CHECK

Check your comprehension by answering these questions.

1. See if you can list four components of emotion:_____
_____ .

2. Injection of the hormone adrenaline in laboratory subjects produces nonemotional physiological changes, described as:

   a. cold emotions *b.* cognitive emotions *c.* cognitive arousal *d.* modulations

3. According to the James-Lange theory of emotion, we see a bear, are frightened, and run.   T or F?

4. The Cannon-Bard theory of emotion says that bodily arousal and emotional experience occur _____
_____ .

5. According to Schachter's cognitive theory, bodily arousal must be labeled or interpreted for an emotional experience to occur.   T or F?

6. The example of the man who thought he was depressed when he was actually ill demonstrates the concept of attribution.   T or F?

7. Subjects in Valins' false heart rate study attributed apparent increases in their heart rate to the action of a placebo.   T or F?

Answers: 1. subjective feelings, emotional expressions, physiological changes, interpretation 2. a 3. F 4. at the same time 5. T 6. T, he attributed his feelings to his stressful circumstances 7. F.

SUGGESTIONS FOR FURTHER READING

Darwin, C. *The Expression of Emotions in Man and Animals*. Chicago University Press, 1965 (first published in 1872).

Kübler-Ross, E. *On Death and Dying*. Macmillan, 1969.

Mandler, G. "Emotion." In *New Directions in Psychology*, **1**, Holt, 1962.

Mark, V. H., and F. R. Ervin. *Violence and the Brain*. Harper & Row, 1970.

McGee, M. G., and M. Snyder. "Attribution and Behavior: Two Field Studies," *Journal of Personality and Social Psychology*, **32**, 1975, pp. 185–190.

Seligman, M., "Fall into Helplessness," *Psychology Today (June)* 1973, pp. 43–48.

Schachter, S., and J. E. Singer. "Cognitive, Social, and Physiological Determinants of the Emotional State," *Psychological Review*, **69**, 1962, pp. 379–399.

Of course you have not read the chapter, you have only surveyed it; but see how well you can do on these questions. Check the answers you think are correct:

1. The purpose of the chapter you surveyed is to:
   - Prove that voodoo can cause death   ☐ Go to **7**.
   - Show that there are several theories dealing with the origins and interpretations of emotions   ☐ Go to **8**.
   - Discuss parts of emotion, theories of emotion, and arousal of emotions   ☐ Go to **9**.

2. The chapter has the following study aids which can help explain the chapter's purpose:
   - Chapter preview, headings, subheadings, questions and answers, definition of words, a learning check, a bibliography   ☐ Go to **10**.
   - Headings, subheadings, italicized words, charts, study questions, summary   ☐ Go to **11**.

I have a choice of two speed reading courses. In one I learn to read really fast but I won't understand it at all, and in the other I'll have complete comprehension reading a page a week

Like the man who slapped the laughing fortune teller, you have to hit a happy medium.

7————————————

You must not have gone beyond the first page. True, voodoo death is mentioned, but only in relation to dealing with emotional actions and reactions. Take another minute to survey the chapter again. Then try another answer in **6**.

8————————————

Close, but not entirely correct. The chapter segment does discuss several theories dealing with emotions, but that's not all.

Try another answer in **6**.

9————————————

Either you lucked out or you used your head! Anyway, you know now that this portion of the chapter on emotions will discuss the parts of an emotion, theories of emotion, and arousal of emotions. That's more than you'd know if you just started reading the chapter straight through and got bogged down in all the terms. You know what to expect and what to look for when you start to study read. You might want to read the chapter in three parts, stopping at the end of each part to make certain you understand what you read before going on.

Now answer Question 2 in **6**.

10————————————

Good. You noticed the aids used in the chapter. More will be said about how to use these later. At least now you are aware of what the chapter is about and how it is set up for you to read.

Go to **12**.

11————————————

Sorry, you goofed. You won't find any charts or summary in this part of the chapter. Look again if you don't believe it.

Then go to **12**.

12————————————

To show you better how survey works, go get a textbook that you are using in one of your classes. That's right. Get it now. Put a book marker here until you return. All this will still be here when you get back.

Are you back with the textbook? Good. Using the following checklist, **survey** a chapter from the book which you have not read yet, preferably one you have been assigned to read. Fill in the title of the chapter and then place a check mark beside each item your textbook has:

Chapter Title ——————————————————————

☐ 1. Headings
☐ 2. Subheadings
☐ 3. Summary
☐ 4. Pictures

☐ 5. Graphs and charts
☐ 6. Other illustrations
☐ 7. Bibliography
☐ 8. Other aids not mentioned (specify what):

_____

_____

In the space provided, write a short paragraph which reflects what you now know about the chapter that you didn't know before.

If, after surveying this chapter, your comprehension and concentration isn't improved when you read the chapter closely, you have permission to call the authors of this book nasty names.

Before going on to the next step of the **SQ3R** study-reading formula, let's check to see how well you understand the surveying process.

- If you are a "super" student, go to **13**.
- If you are a "get-by" student, go to **14**.

13————————————————

Hi Superstud(ent). In the blank spaces below, write the steps for surveying a **textbook** in the proper order.

1. _____

2. _____

3. _____

4. _____

5. _____

Check your answers on **15**.

14————————————

In the blank spaces provided, write the steps for surveying a **chapter** in the proper order.

1. ————————————

2. ————————————

3. ————————————

4. ————————————

5. ————————————

Check your answers on **16**.

15————————————

You should have listed the following steps for surveying a textbook:
1. Read the preface and introduction.
2. Read the table of contents.
3. Check for visual aids.
4. Check for reference works and glossaries.
5. Read the summaries.

If you were correct, go to **14**.
If you missed any one of these or missed the order, return to **5** and read it again. Perhaps you listed the steps for surveying a chapter instead of the steps for a book.
When you understand the order, go to **14**.

16————————————

You should have listed the following steps for surveying a chapter:

1. Read the title and let it "sink" in.
2. Read the headings and subheadings.
3. Read the summary.
4. Read the captions.
5. Check for a bibliography.

If you were correct, go to **18**.

If you missed any one of these or missed the order, return to **6** and read it again.

When you understand the order, go to **18**.

17————————————————————————

What are you doing here? There were no directions sending you here. Scat! Go back to the last frame you read and find out where you belong.

18————————————————————————

Q = Question

The second step of the SQ3R study-reading formula is **question**. You probably know already that we can remember something much better if it has some specific meaning for us. That's why reading an assigned chapter from a textbook simply because the instructor said to read it is not always a meaningful experience. If you have no real purpose for reading something—other than that it was assigned—you will get little meaningful comprehension.

The best way to get more from reading assignments is to ask yourself **questions** about what you are going to read. Questions aid study reading because they focus attention on the subject matter. They provide a personal purpose for reading—a purpose beyond the fact the material is assigned. Looking for answers to questions also keeps the mind from wandering to other things as we read and therefore speeds up the studying process.

Surveying, if done properly, provides a natural setting for asking questions. Here are some examples of the kinds of questions you might ask yourself while surveying or after surveying. *Learn them; they are important.*

1. What does the title of the chapter mean?
2. What do I already know about the subject?
3. What did my instructor say about this chapter or subject when it was assigned? [She (or he) may have said something in class or on a handout sheet.]
4. What questions do the *headings* and *subheadings* suggest? (Some study-skills experts recommend that you turn the chapter title and headings into questions.) For example, you might have asked when you started reading this section, "What does the **Q = Question** mean?"

5. Are there questions at the beginning or end of the chapter? (These questions are often skipped by students when they should be read carefully since they ask what the author obviously thinks is important.)

6. Are there questions in the workbook that may go with the textbook? (Often workbooks accompany textbooks and contain questions related to the chapter assigned. Make good use of such aids.)

7. What do I want to know about the contents of this chapter when I am finished reading?

Now look over the questions once again and make certain you know them and understand them.

Go to **19**.

19————————————————

Practice is what makes a skill perfect—provided it's the right kind of practice. So, once again it is time to practice what you just learned. Turn back to the sample chapter from a psychology textbook you surveyed a few pages back. (It begins on page 99.) Pretend you have to read the chapter for a psychology class that you are taking. This time follow the steps for surveying and questioning *together*. Right now, you are only *preparing* to read it. You will notice that not all of the sample questions listed in **18** can be applied to this "pretend" assignment, but at least see what kinds of questions you can come up with.

Ready? Back to the sample chapter and try what you just learned. Then come back here.

Fine. Now check your technique by turning the following headings from the chapter into questions that could guide your reading. In the space provided, write in what you think are good questions to ask yourself while reading that section in the chapter. Try using *who, what, why, when, where, how, why not,* and *how come* as starters.

1. "Emotion" (the title of the chapter) _____

_____

_____

2. "Parts of an Emotion" _____

_____

_____

3. "Theories of Emotion—Four Ways to Fear a Bear" _____

_____

_____

4. "Attribution" _____

_____

_____

Check your answers by comparing them with the following. The wording may be different but the ideas should be close.

1. What will I learn about emotion? What emotions will be discussed? What causes emotion? Is emotion physical or mental? How can emotion be physical?
2. Can an emotion have parts? What is meant by "parts of an emotion"? How can emotion be divided?
3. What does "Four Ways To Fear a Bear" mean? Will fear be used as an example of emotion? Will four theories of emotion be covered?
4. What is attribution? How is it connected to fear? Where does the word "attribution" come from?

If you had these questions or ones like them, go to **20**.
If you had trouble understanding what was meant by **Q = Questioning**, read **18** again and pay attention to the way the questions listed came from the headings in the sample psychology textbook chapter. Then go to **20**.

20————————————————————

Is that textbook you were using before still near? Get it again, please. Then open it to the chapter you surveyed and answer each of the following questions in the spaces provided.

Title of Book _____ Author _____
Title of Chapter _____

1. What does the title of the chapter mean?

_____

_____

2. What do I already know about the subject?

   a. _____

   b. _____

   c. _____

3. What did my instructor say about this chapter or subject when it was assigned?

_____

_____

4. What questions do the headings and subheadings suggest?

   a. _____

   b. _____

   c. _____

5. Are there questions at the beginning or end of the chapter? _____
Did you read them? _____

6. Are there questions in the workbook? (This may not apply to your book.) _____ Did you read them? _____

7. What do I want to know about the contents of this chapter when I am finished reading?

   a. _____

   b. _____

   c. _____

What you just did probably seemed like a time-consuming job. Remember, however, that while you were asked to do this in writing now, you will be doing this mentally as you survey. Right now these steps may take more time than they will later, but that's because you are in the process of learning. The actual time it takes to survey and question is really a matter of a few minutes. These few minutes will be well worth the better comprehension you will receive in the long run.

Go to 21.

21————————————————————

Here's a quick review before going to the next step of the **SQ3R** method.

A. **SQ3R** stands for (fill in the blanks).

S _____

Q _____
[1]R _____

[2]R _____

[3]R _____

Turn to **22** for the answer.

B. List the five steps for surveying a **chapter**.

1. _____
2. _____
3. _____
4. _____
5. _____

Turn to **23** for the answer.

C. List the types of **questions** you should ask yourself as you survey.

1. _____
2. _____
3. _____
4. _____
5. _____
6. _____
7. _____

Turn to **24** to check your answers.

22-_____

Survey, Question, Read, Recite, Review
   If you were correct, pat yourself on the back and then answer B in **21**.

If you missed any one of these steps, return to page 93 and reread the explanation. It is important that you memorize the correct order of the **SQ3R** formula. Then answer B in **21**.

23————————————————————

Your answers should be in the following order:

1. Read the title and let it "sink" in.
2. Read the headings and subheadings.
3. Read the summary.
4. Read the captions.
5. Check for a bibliography.

If you were correct, smile loudly and go to question C in **21**.
If you missed any part of the question, return to **6** and read the section **Surveying a Chapter**. Learn those five points well. Then answer C in **21**.

24————————————————————

Your answers should be in the following order:

1. What does the title of the chapter mean?
2. What do I already know about the subject?
3. What did my instructor say about the chapter when it was assigned?
4. What questions do the headings and subheadings suggest?
5. Are there questions at the beginning or end of the chapter?
6. Are there questions in an accompanying workbook?
7. What do I want to know about the contents of the chapter when I am finished?

If you answered all of these correctly, sigh in relief and go to **25**.
If you goofed, return to **18** and read it again.
When you can correctly answer question C, go to **25**.

25————————————————————

R^1 = Read

The third step of the **SQ3R** formula is to **read**. Too many students begin reading an assignment without any preparations such as the survey and questions steps. The results are usually poor comprehension, mind wandering, and lots of re-reading of parts that don't make sense. It is true that your assignment is to be read, but not without the proper preparation that the S and Q techniques offer. The actual close reading of the material will be easier and comprehension will be better after you have prepared.

Here is how you should do your close reading (R^1 = **Read**). **Learn these steps. They are important to remember.**

Step 1   Read to *answer the questions* you raised while doing the survey/question routine; or read to answer the questions at the beginning or end of the chapter if there are any. Remember, reading to answer these questions gives you a purpose and a sense of direction.

Step 2   Read all the *added attractions* in the chapter. Most textbooks have pictures, maps, graphs, tables, and other illustrations which supplement or clarify what the author is saying.

Step 3   Read extra carefully all the *underlined, italicized, or bold printed words or phrases*. When terms are printed in different size type, it means the author is calling attention to them. Study such terms carefully. Usually they are quiz or test items.

Read the three points above again. Make certain you know them.

Now return to the sample textbook chapter on psychology in **6**.

You have already applied the survey/question techniques, but you may want to S/Q again. This time apply Step 3, R^1 = **Read**, looking for answers to questions you raised.

When you have finished, go to **26**.

26————————————————————

If you have finished using R^1 = **Read** on the sample chapter, answer the following question so you can see how well you read.

Check the appropriate answer.

Question 1   According to the chapter you read, emotional experiences:

(a) Are basically subjective feelings   ☐ See **27**.
(b) Have a number of parts   ☐ See **28**.
(c) Don't know   ☐ See **29**.

CENTER FOR TEACHING AND LEARNING
P. O. Box H
Stanford, California 94305

27————————————————————

If you selected this answer, you misread somewhere. If you looked under the heading "Parts of an Emotion" (that in itself should have helped you answer), you will notice that it states: "There are a number of facets to any emotional experience." Following the opening paragraph there are four subheadings, all parts of an emotional experience.

Go back to **26** and read the other answer. Then go to **28**.

28————————————————————

Well done. There is a heading entitled "Parts of an Emotion" and then four subheadings discussing various facets of an emotional experience.

Now try Question 2 in **30**.

29————————————————————

At least you're honest. Read the section in the psych chapter under the heading "Parts of an Emotion" and try again, picking a different answer in **26**.

30————————————————————

Question 2   What causes emotion?

(a) No one knows for certain; there are several
theories.   ☐ See **31**.
(b) There are four major theories about what takes
place when a person experiences an emotion.   ☐ See **32**.

31————————————————————

You aren't wrong, but you aren't right enough. It's true that more than one theory is discussed in the chapter, but if you read both answer choices (and didn't guess), then (b) is the better answer because four major theories are presented, not several. (Always read all choices on a test before making a selection.)

Review the selection under the heading "Theories of Emotion: Four Ways to Fear a Bear," and then go to **33**.

32————————————————

Good—if you didn't guess. The second choice is more specific than the first.

Go on to **33**.

33————————————————

Question 3 Which of the following theories of emotion is considered wrong?

(a) The Commonsense Theory of Emotion   ☐ See **34**.
(b) The James-Lange Theory   ☐ See **35**.
(c) The Cannon-Bard Theory   ☐ See **36**.

34————————————————

You're a smartie! Move on to Question 4 in **37**.

35————————————————

Negative, my friend. You're getting something confused. Skim over the section dealing with emotional theories for the correct answer, and then try **33** again.

36————————————————

Read what **35** has to say and do it. You have some theories crossed up somewhere.

37————————————————

Question 4 Injection of the hormone adrenaline in laboratory subjects produces nonemotional physiological changes described as:

(a) Cognitive emotions   ☐ See **38**.
(b) Cold emotions   ☐ See **39**.
(c) Attribution   ☐ See **40**.

38————————————————

Cognitive emotions, you say? Well, you're wrong.

   First of all, if you did the Learning Check section when you read the psych chapter, you would have already answered this question. It was in the quiz you were supposed to take.

   Second, if you carefully read the section under the subheading "Interpretation," the term "cold emotions" is used and defined. Reread that section, and then go back to **37** and try again.

39————————————————

Did you get this correct because it was one of the Learning Check questions in the sample chapter? Aids in learning such as these can be very helpful when study reading. Teachers often base test questions on questions in the book.

   OK. Go on to **41**.

40————————————————

Hmm. Now how did you come up with this? Go back to the subheading "Interpretation" and try another answer in **37** when finished.

41————————————————

Once more, get that textbook you have been practicing with. Select a chapter you have not read yet and practice using the survey/question technique. In the spaces below, answer the following items:

1. Chapter title ————————————————————
2. What are some questions the title raises or that you want answered?

   a. ————————————————————————
   b. ————————————————————————
   c. ————————————————————————

3. What subjects do the headings deal with?

   a. ————————————————————————
   b. ————————————————————————
   c. ————————————————————————

4. What do you already know about these subjects?

   a. _____

   b. _____

   c. _____

5. What do you want to know when you finish reading this chapter?

   a. _____

   b. _____

   c. _____

Now read the chapter from your textbook following the three points mentioned under R^1 = **Read**. Then return to the following paragraph.

If you are finished reading the chapter from your textbook, answer the following questions.

1. Write the answers to the questions you wrote down under Item 2.

   a. _____

   b. _____

   c. _____

2. Write down one thing you learned about each of the subjects you wrote down under Item 3.

   a. _____

   b. _____

   c. _____

3. Did you find answers for each point you listed under Item 5?

   a. _____

   b. _____

   c. _____

We can't help you with your answers, but at least we helped you to apply what you are learning in this book to an actual textbook for one of your classes. Remember to keep trying these methods on your actual assignments.

Now go on to **42**.

42————————————————————

R^2 = Recite

The fourth step of the **SQ3R** study formula is **recite**. For the purposes of this formula, **recite** means to go over what you read in step 3 (R^1 = **Read**) by either orally summarizing what you just read, or by making notes of some type. Studies reveal that students tend to forget as much as 80 percent of what they learned from reading *within 2 weeks after studying!* On the other hand, when students recited immediately after reading, they forgot only 20 percent during the same time period. It is a known fact that recitation reinforces what you read, helps you to see what mistakes you may have made when you read it the first time (R^1 = **Read**).

Here are a few "don'ts" when you do the R^2 = **Recite** step.

1. Don't stop to recite after every paragraph or two. This will break the continuity of the section you are reading.
2. Don't wait to recite if a section from one heading to another is too long. You should use your own judgment about places to stop and recite.
3. Don't underline long passages. It is better to be selective and mark only key ideas or terms.
4. Don't use ink to mark your book unless you don't make mistakes. You can erase pencil marks.
5. Don't underline or mark as you read; mark only *after* you have read the passage and understand it.

If you follow this advice, you will find your marks are more meaningful when you review for a test weeks or months later.

Return now to that old familiar sample chapter from a psychology text in **6**. You applied R^1 = **Read** to it already. This time return to the subheading "Theories of Emotion—" and apply R^2 = **Recite** to it. Then return here again.

If you forgot or neglected to orally recite after reading, see **43**.

If you remembered to recite orally, write a summary in the space below of what you orally recited when you finished the section "Theories of Emotion."

Summary of "Theories of Emotion"

Now go to **44** and compare your summary with it.

43————————————————————

Shame on you. How are you going to be a better student if you don't try what you are learning? Go back to **42** and in your own words orally recite what you think the section was about. Then in the space provided in **42** write a summary of your oral recitation.

44————————————————————

Compare your summary with this one. Naturally, wording will be different, but the main ideas should be contained in your summary. We have underlined key words and phrases for you to see if you've included most of them in your summary:

> There are <u>four major theories</u> about what takes place when a person experiences an emotion. The <u>Commonsense Theory</u> says, "We see a bear, are frightened, and run." But this theory is <u>too simple</u> for psychologists. The <u>James-Lange Theory</u> says emotion is <u>bodily arousal</u>, meaning the body must be aroused before an emotion is experienced. <u>The Cannon-Bard Theory</u> says emotions come from <u>the brain</u>, causing <u>emotional feelings</u> and <u>bodily experiences</u> to <u>occur together</u>. The fourth theory, <u>Schachter's Cognitive Theory</u>, claims emotion is <u>a combination of physical arousal</u> and the <u>label</u> given the emotion. For instance, you see a bear, you are aroused by how the bear seems—friendly or mean. <u>Attribution</u> refers to perceiving an emotion <u>based</u> on what <u>feelings of physical arousal are attributed</u> to.

Make certain your summary covers the four major theories *and* attribution. If your summary does not contain these elements, go to **45**. If your summary compares well, go to **46**.

45————————————————————

You might have had trouble with your summary because you were not paying attention to the clues given in the chapter. The heading "Theories of Emotion: Four Ways to Fear a Bear" should have raised some questions: How many theories of emotion are there? Does "Four Ways to Fear a Bear" mean there are four theories? What is a theory of emotion? As you read to find answers, you should have noticed each of the four theories plus attribution has its own subheading. It's often a good idea to read from heading to heading, stopping to make sure you understand what you just read before going on.

Go back to the "Theories of Emotion" section. Read each subheaded section listed below and write in the definition for each:

1. The Commonsense Theory of Emotion

   _____

   _____

2. The James-Lange Theory

   _____

   _____

3. The Cannon-Bard Theory

   _____

   _____

4. Schachter's Cognitive Theory of Emotion

   _____

   _____

5. Attribution

   _____

   _____

Now rewrite your summary of these main points below:

Compare your paragraph with the example in **44**. Then go on to **46**.

46————————————————

If you applied the correct procedure for R^2 = **Recite**, you marked or underlined the section "Theories of Emotion" as you recited. If you did *NOT* mark or underline, go to **47**. If you *did* mark or underline when you applied R^2 = **Recite, go to 48**.

47————————————————

Are you stubborn or did you forget to mark and underline as you recited? We suggest you go back to **42** and start all over. This time, pay attention to the steps involved in R^2 = **Recite** and the reasons for them.

48————————————————

There is not enough space in this book to give you sample markings for comparison of the entire section you marked. However, Figure B is a one-page reproduction of part of the section you marked. Compare your markings with Figure B. Notice the following points:

1. The page has not been overmarked.
2. Numbers are used in the margin to designate the theories of emotion being discussed.
3. Key phrases are circled; detailed points are underlined.
4. Points needed for a quick review before a test are all marked for special attention.
5. A brief summary is written at the end of the section.

If you did not mark as shown in Figure B, re-read the steps for R^2 = **Recite** again and also study Figure B carefully.

If your markings look like ours, go on to **49**, R^3 = **Review**.

49————————————————

R^3 = Review

The fifth and last step of the **SQ3R** study formula is to **review**. Most students do review what they have read just before taking a test. But there is more to it than that. **Reviewing** should combine the use of the total **SQ3R** formula. It consists of surveying what you have read again, only this time you already know what the material is; and you are surveying to see what you remember about the title, headings, and subheadings. It also consists of using your notes or markings to refresh your memory regarding the key points you already found when you read and recited.

Here are the proper steps for **Review**. **Learn them**.

1. **Review immediately** after reading a chapter. This means reading over your notes or markings and putting together all the different sections of the chapter so you have a total picture of what you read. This immediate review will be fairly short because everything will be fresh in your mind.
2. **Review weekly**. After you have read other chapters and a week has passed, go back and review earlier chapters so that you can get a picture of the progress the textbook is making.
3. **Plan a final review** before taking an exam on the subject. Plan ahead so that you have time to do a careful, thorough review.

If you are a "get-by" student, go to **50**.
If you are a "super" student, go to **51**.

50————————————————

About all we can say now is try the **SQ3R** system on some of your textbooks. Take what you've learned here and use it. Books vary, so feel free to "bend" the formula and the steps in it to fit your particular book. Thousands of students have pulled their grades up by using the **SQ3R** formula. When you first use it, you may find yourself concentrating too much on how to use it, rather than on what you are reading. Don't worry about it and *don't blame the formula*. A little practice and you will be using the formula steps without thinking about them. That's when you'll feel the difference. Good luck!

Go to **52**.

51————————————————

Glad to have you back. Here's a chance for you to see if all you have been learning really pays off. Once again, return to the sample psychology chapter and review it. Then answer the following questions about the chapter. Circle the correct response.

Figure B*

1. **The Commonsense Theory of Emotion** Common sense tells us that we see a bear, are frightened, and run (and sweat and yell). This explanation is far too simple to satisfy any psychologist. Besides, it is wrong. The theories of emotion that follow show why.

2. **The James-Lange Theory** (1884–1885) In the 1880s, American psychologist William James and Danish psychologist Carl Lange proposed a different version of the relationship between emotional feelings and bodily states. James and Lange suggested that, "we are afraid of a bear because we run, or angry because we strike." In doing so, they turned the tables on our usual conception of emotion. Instead of assuming that bodily changes (such as increased heart rate) *follow* a feeling such as fear, James and Lange assumed that bodily changes *precede* emotion. They argued that we see a bear, run, and *then* become conscious of fear.

To support this line of thought, James pointed out that we often do not experience an emotion until after reacting. For example, imagine that you are driving and that a car suddenly pulls out in front of you. You swerve and skid to an abrupt halt at the side of the road. Only after you have come to a stop do you notice your pounding heart, rapid breathing, and tense muscles—and recognize your fear. The James-Lange theory of emotion may help explain an interesting effect you have probably observed. When you are feeling "down" or sad, forcing yourself to smile will sometimes be followed by an actual improvement in your mood (Laird, 1974).

3. **The Cannon-Bard Theory** (1927) American physiologist Walter Cannon and his student Phillip Bard found a number of reasons to reject the James-Lange theory. While agreeing that the body becomes stirred up during emotion, Cannon and Bard noted that there are only slight differences in the physiology of various emotions. These differences are just not enough to allow for the rich and varied emotional life that humans experience. As a matter of fact, persons with spinal cord injuries still experience emotion, even though they may be unable to feel the normal sensations of bodily arousal (Hohmann, 1966).

Question: How do Cannon and Bard interpret emotion?

For the reasons just stated, and a number of others, Cannon (1932) proposed that emotional feelings and bodily arousal occur at the same time. In this version, seeing a bear activates the cortex, the thalamus, and the hypothalamus of the brain. Cannon believed the thalamus alerts both the hypothalamus and the cortex for action, but before the hypothalamus arouses the body, the cortex must give the go-ahead by deciding that the bear is dangerous. If the bear is seen as dangerous, bodily arousal, running, and feelings of fear will all be generated at the same time by brain activity.

*From Dennis Coon, *Introduction to Psychology: Exploration and Application,* Second Edition, © 1980, West Publishing Company, St. Paul, Minn.

Let's summarize: The common-sense theory of emotion is wrong. The James-Lange theory says emotion *is* bodily arousal and that the body must be aroused *before* an emotion is experienced. The Cannon-Bard theory moved emotions from the body to the head by saying that emotions are organized in the brain and that emotional feelings and bodily expressions occur simultaneously. There is a fourth possibility.

↓

4. Schachter's Cognitive Theory of Emotion (1971) The previous theories are mostly concerned with emotion as physiological response. In Stanley Schachter's view, cognitive (mental) factors are also major determinants of emotions. According to Schachter, emotion is a combination of physical arousal and the *label* that is applied to that arousal.

In other words, Schachter assumes that when people become physically aroused, they have a need to interpret the arousal. The label (such as anger, fear, or happiness) applied to emotional feelings will be influenced by past experiences, the situation in which people find themselves, and the reactions of those around them.

To test this theory, Schachter and Singer (1962) injected subjects with the drug adrenaline. Subjects were misinformed about the drug they were receiving. Instead of adrenaline, they were told that they were receiving a vitamin being tested for its effects on vision. While this vitamin was supposedly taking effect, subjects were asked to wait in a room with another subject. The second "subject" was really an accomplice of the experimenters who was trained to

Four major areas of emotion: (1) commonsense theory (wrong); (2) James Lange theory (body changes precede emotions); Cannon-Bard theory (emotional arousal & body arousal occur together); Schachter's cognitive theory (emotion combination of physical arousal and label).

T/F 1. The four components of emotion are subjective feelings, emotional expression, physiological changes, and interpretation.

T/F 2. Injection of the hormone adrenaline in laboratory subjects produces emotional physiological changes.

T/F 3. According to the James-Lange theory of emotion, we see a bear, are frightened, and run.

T/F 4. The Cannon-Bard theory of emotion says that bodily arousal and emotional experience occur at the same time.

T/F 5. According to Schachter's cognitive theory, bodily arousal must be labeled or interpreted for an emotional experience to occur.

T/F   6. The example of the man who thought he was depressed when he was actually ill demonstrates the conception of attribution.

T/F   7. Subjects in Valins' false heart rate study attributed apparent increases in their heart rate to the action of a placebo.

Compare your answers with these: (1) true; (2) false, nonemotional; (3) false, commonsense theory; (4) true; (5) true; (6) true, he contributed his feelings to his stressful circumstances; (7) false, to perception of emotions.

A good score would be six or more correct. However, if you did the Learning Check in the chapter when you read it, you should have gotten all answers correct. These are the same questions!

Go back to **50** now.

52——————————————

Many students *cram* before an exam. Sometimes the results are good— *for that particular test*. However, most often the results of cramming are disastrous. We don't recommend it. But if you are going to cram, at least use part of the **SQ3R** formula we've been dealing with so far—R^2 = **Recite**. Assuming you have read the chapters you are to be tested on, it will be to your advantage to get together with a friend or two and orally recite to one another. Try these steps:

1. Ask each other what the titles of chapters really mean.
2. Ask each other to explain what the headings and subheadings in the chapter mean.
3. Ask each other to define italicized or bold print words or terms.
4. Ask each other questions based on tables, charts, pictures, etc. in the chapters.
5. Ask each other what types of questions you think the instructor will ask on the test.
6. If there are questions at the end of the chapters, or if the instructor gave out a handout sheet with questions, try answering them in your own words.
7. Don't wait until the last minute to do your cramming. Get a good night's rest.

Recitation helps you organize your thoughts, forces you to put your thoughts into words, and helps you remember things longer. But a one-shot cramming scene before a test will tend to confuse you and jam up your mind. If you do cram and pass the test, chances are you will forget it all in a matter of days or even hours. If that's the type of education you want, you're welcome to it.

Enough lecturing. Time to move on to other things. BUT!!.... **DON'T FORGET TO SQ3R**.

PRACTICE PAGES FOR SURVEYING A *TEXTBOOK*

There are four worksheets, all the same, on the following pages. Use them in the following way:

1. Select a textbook you are currently using in a class you are taking.
2. Use one of the following worksheets from this book.
3. Answer the questions on the worksheet by using the text you selected.
4. Do the same for the remaining worksheets.
5. Follow the same routine on your own even after the worksheets are used up.

Surveying Your Textbook

1. Name of textbook: _____

2. List at least three questions or thoughts which the title suggests to you:

   a. _____

   b. _____

   c. _____

3. List at least two major points the author makes in the Preface:

   a. _____

   b. _____

4. List at least two major points the author makes in the Introduction:

   a. _____

   b. _____

5. Take at least five chapter titles listed in the Table of Contents and turn them into questions:

   a. _____

   b. _____

   c. _____

   d. _____

   e. _____

6. If there is an Appendix, what does it contain?

   _____

   _____

   _____

7. Does the book contain a Glossary? _____ An Index? _____ If the answers are yes, look over the Glossary and/or thumb through the Index looking for familiar names, places, or terms. How much do you think you are going to know about the contents?

   _____

   _____

8. Look through the first two chapters of the book and check any of the following aids used in them:

_____ Headings	_____ Study questions
_____ Subheadings	_____ Assignments
_____ Italics	_____ Pictures
_____ Summary	_____ Graphs, charts
_____ Footnotes	_____ Other: _____
_____ Bibliography	

9. Write a short statement regarding your hopes, fears, expectations, etc., about the book:

Surveying Your Textbook

1. Name of textbook: _____

2. List at least three questions or thoughts which the title suggests to you:

   a. _____

   b. _____

   c. _____

3. List at least two major points the author makes in the Preface:

   a. _____

   b. _____

4. List at least two major points the author makes in the Introduction:

   a. _____

   b. _____

5. Take at least five chapter titles listed in the Table of Contents and turn them into questions:

   a. _____

   b. _____

   c. _____

   d. _____

   e. _____

6. If there is an Appendix, what does it contain?

   _____

   _____

   _____

7. Does the book contain a Glossary? _____ An Index? _____ If the answers are yes, look over the Glossary and/or thumb through the Index looking for familiar names, places, or terms. How much do you think you are going to know about the contents?

   _____

   _____

8. Look through the first two chapters of the book and check any of the following aids used in them:

____ Headings	____ Study questions
____ Subheadings	____ Assignments
____ Italics	____ Pictures
____ Summary	____ Graphs, charts
____ Footnotes	____ Other: _____
____ Bibliography	

9. Write a short statement regarding your hopes, fears, expectations, etc., about the book:

Surveying Your Textbook

1. Name of textbook: _____

2. List at least three questions or thoughts which the title suggests to you:

   a. _____

   b. _____

   c. _____

3. List at least two major points the author makes in the Preface:

   a. _____

   b. _____

4. List at least two major points the author makes in the Introduction:

   a. _____

   b. _____

5. Take at least five chapter titles listed in the Table of Contents and turn them into questions:

   a. _____

   b. _____

   c. _____

   d. _____

   e. _____

6. If there is an Appendix, what does it contain?

   _____

   _____

   _____

7. Does the book contain a Glossary? _____ An Index? _____ If the answers are yes, look over the Glossary and/or thumb through the Index looking for familiar names, places, or terms. How much do you think you are going to know about the contents?

   _____

   _____

8. Look through the first two chapters of the book and check any of the following aids used in them:

____ Headings	____ Study questions
____ Subheadings	____ Assignments
____ Italics	____ Pictures
____ Summary	____ Graphs, charts
____ Footnotes	____ Other: _____
____ Bibliography	

9. Write a short statement regarding your hopes, fears, expectations, etc., about the book:

Surveying Your Textbook

1. Name of textbook: _____

2. List at least three questions or thoughts which the title suggests to you:

   a. _____

   b. _____

   c. _____

3. List at least two major points the author makes in the Preface:

   a. _____

   b. _____

4. List at least two major points the author makes in the Introduction:

   a. _____

   b. _____

5. Take at least five chapter titles listed in the Table of Contents and turn them into questions:

   a. _____

   b. _____

   c. _____

   d. _____

   e. _____

6. If there is an Appendix, what does it contain?

   _____

   _____

   _____

7. Does the book contain a Glossary? _____ An Index? _____ If the answers are yes, look over the Glossary and/or thumb through the Index looking for familiar names, places, or terms. How much do you think you are going to know about the contents?

   _____

   _____

8. Look through the first two chapters of the book and check any of the following aids used in them:

_____ Headings		_____ Study questions	
_____ Subheadings		_____ Assignments	
_____ Italics		_____ Pictures	
_____ Summary		_____ Graphs, charts	
_____ Footnotes		_____ Other: _____	
_____ Bibliography			

9. Write a short statement regarding your hopes, fears, expectations, etc., about the book:

PRACTICE PAGES FOR SURVEYING A
TEXTBOOK CHAPTER

There are four worksheets on the following pages. Use them in the following way:

1. Select a textbook you are using in a class you are taking, preferably a book which you are having trouble reading.
2. Use one of the following worksheets from this book.
3. Answer the questions on the worksheet by using a chapter you have not read in the book you have selected.
4. Do the same for the remaining worksheets.
5. Follow the same routine on other chapters even after the worksheets are used up.

Surveying a Textbook Chapter

1. Name of the textbook: _____

2. Chapter title: _____

3. List at least three questions the title suggests to you:

   a. _____

   b. _____

   c. _____

4. Read the first paragraph, each bold heading and subheading, and the last two paragraphs of the chapter. What is the chapter about?

   _____

   _____

   _____

5. How much do you already know about the subject?

   _____

   _____

6. What study aids does the chapter contain?

   ____ Bold print   ____ Summary
   ____ Italicized words   ____ Bibliography
   ____ Graphs, charts, etc.   ____ Questions
   ____ Pictures   ____ Other: _____

7. How long will it take you to study this chapter? _____

8. If you will need to divide the chapter up into sections to study it, where are you going to divide it? (Name page numbers)

   _____

9. List at least four questions you are going to read to find answers to:

   a. _____

   b. _____

   c. _____

   d. _____

Surveying a Textbook Chapter

1. Name of the textbook: _____

2. Chapter title: _____

3. List at least three questions the title suggests to you:

   a. _____

   b. _____

   c. _____

4. Read the first paragraph, each bold heading and subheading, and the last two paragraphs of the chapter. What is the chapter about?

   _____

   _____

   _____

5. How much do you already know about the subject?

   _____

   _____

6. What study aids does the chapter contain?

   _____ Bold print   _____ Summary
   _____ Italicized words   _____ Bibliography
   _____ Graphs, charts, etc. _____ Questions
   _____ Pictures   _____ Other: _____

7. How long will it take you to study this chapter? _____

8. If you will need to divide the chapter up into sections to study it, where are you going to divide it? (Name page numbers)

   _____

9. List at least four questions you are going to read to find answers to:

   a. _____

   b. _____

   c. _____

   d. _____

Surveying a Textbook Chapter

1. Name of the textbook: _____

2. Chapter title: _____

3. List at least three questions the title suggests to you:

   a. _____

   b. _____

   c. _____

4. Read the first paragraph, each bold heading and subheading, and the last two paragraphs of the chapter. What is the chapter about?

   _____

   _____

   _____

5. How much do you already know about the subject?

   _____

   _____

6. What study aids does the chapter contain?

   _____ Bold print   _____ Summary
   _____ Italicized words   _____ Bibliography
   _____ Graphs, charts, etc.   _____ Questions
   _____ Pictures   _____ Other: _____

7. How long will it take you to study this chapter? _____

8. If you will need to divide the chapter up into sections to study it, where are you going to divide it? (Name page numbers)

   _____

9. List at least four questions you are going to read to find answers to:

   a. _____

   b. _____

   c. _____

   d. _____

Surveying a Textbook Chapter

1. Name of the textbook: _____

2. Chapter title: _____

3. List at least three questions the title suggests to you:

   a. _____

   b. _____

   c. _____

4. Read the first paragraph, each bold heading and subheading, and the last two paragraphs of the chapter. What is the chapter about?

   _____

   _____

   _____

5. How much do you already know about the subject?

   _____

   _____

6. What study aids does the chapter contain?

   _____ Bold print   _____ Summary
   _____ Italicized words   _____ Bibliography
   _____ Graphs, charts, etc.   _____ Questions
   _____ Pictures   _____ Other: _____

7. How long will it take you to study this chapter? _____

8. If you will need to divide the chapter up into sections to study it, where are you going to divide it? (Name page numbers)

   _____

9. List at least four questions you are going to read to find answers to:

   a. _____

   b. _____

   c. _____

   d. _____

CHAPTER FIVE
Writing Short Papers

GOALS AND OBJECTIVES

General Goals   When you complete this unit, you will

1. Believe that there is a general approach to writing short papers
2. Learn how to apply a systematic procedure for more effective essay writing
3. Have increased confidence in writing short essays

Specific Objectives   When you complete this unit, you will

1. Recall the meaning of **SLOWER**
2. Adopt the **SLOWER** formula for writing short essays
3. Select and narrow down a topic appropriate for short essays
4. List and order the component parts of a short essay before writing it
5. Examine the first draft for errors in grammar, spelling, punctuation, and paragraph control
6. Revise the first draft on the basis of any errors uncovered

"A 500-word paper on hickory nut hunting? That's the silliest assignment I've ever heard of! I've never even seen a hickory nut, for crying out loud. How am I going to write a paper on something I don't know anything about?" moans the student.

Ah, the lament of the poor, tortured student. The terrible, terrible things he must suffer to get his degree.

Well, if you've ever been faced with a similar ordeal, you know you have at least three choices. You can drop the class and hope you "luck out" with a different instructor; or you can cheat and pay someone else to write a paper for you (that would at least lower the nation's unemployment somewhat); or you must learn to accept such assignments as a matter of course and buckle down to it. Let's assume you bought this book for the third reason.

We can't promise to teach you how to write an A paper on hickory nut hunting, but we can teach you some methods that are used by successful students and writers.

If you want help with writing better essays, go to **1** now.

If you don't need help in writing papers, go find someone else who does and give him a hand—and then go on to the next chapter.

1————————————————

Let's pretend.

You are now sitting in an English composition class, and your instructor has told you to write a short paper on a poem you were supposed to read before coming to class.

Let's also pretend that you did read the poem. So you get out some notebook paper and start writing. You get your name and date on the paper when suddenly . . . a blank mind! You can't think of anything to write.

There are six general steps to writing essays that can make writing papers easier and faster. These steps have been combined into a formula called, oddly enough, **SLOWER**.

SLOWER is a mnemonic device (memory aid) designed to help you remember the six steps for good essay writing.

Learn to use these six steps in order, and you'll find **SLOWER** to be faster in the long run.

S = **Select** a topic you can handle
L = **List** all your ideas related to the topic
O = **Order** your ideas
W = **Write** a first draft
E = **Examine** your draft for errors
R = **Revise** before turning in the final paper

It is important that you remember each of the six steps in their proper order. Once you learn in more detail what these steps are and how to use them, you can modify them to fit your needs. But for now, *reread the* **SLOWER** *formula above.*

Then go to **2**.

2————————————

Without referring back, write in what each letter stands for.

S = _____

L = _____

O = _____

W = _____

E = _____

R = _____

Check your answers by comparing what you have written with the explanation in **1**.

If you made any mistakes, stop now and learn the **SLOWER** formula before going to **3**.

If you made no errors, go to **3** with a grin on your face.

3————————————

S = Select a topic you can handle.

This first step in the **SLOWER** formula may seem obvious, but unfortunately many students do not give it enough consideration. Here are some helpful points regarding the proper selection of a topic.

(a) <u>Select a topic that is interesting to you, if possible.</u> Most instructors look for originality; so you should attempt to substitute your own topics for suggestions whenever you can. If you're interested in the topic, you'll *want* to do the paper.

(b) <u>Select a topic your instructor is interested in, whenever possible.</u> It never hurts to please! And it's not "brown nosing" as long as it is a topic that also interests you.

(c) <u>Select a topic that is not too technical and does not require extensive research</u>. Any topic that requires lots of reading or documentation should be saved for a research paper. (See Chapter 6.)

(d) <u>Select a topic from daily experience</u>. You have a lot to write when you stop to think about it. Don't be afraid to share your experiences in your papers—experiences such as all the "hang-ups" in registering for classes, walking along the beach in the early morning, the old grump who gave you a bad time at the store, the feelings you had watching your girl (or your boyfriend) in a play, a comparison of two things (such as the similarities and differences between your mother and your father), or a contrast of two things (such as the differences between a VW and a Chevy you once owned), and on and on.

(e) <u>When you can't think of a topic, thumb through the index of a book in a subject you like</u>. Ideas based on various entries should start developing in your mind. Of course, this doesn't mean you copy your paper from a book. It just means that you are going to use the *ideas* from the book.

(f) <u>Once you've selected a topic, get started on it right away</u>. Don't put it off.

To help you remember what you just read, fill in the spaces below with the correct key words. If you need to, review the above points for the answers.

(a) Select a topic that is _____ to you, if possible.

(b) Select a topic your _____ is interested in.

(c) Select a topic that is not _____ _____ and does

not require _____ _____ .

(d) Select a topic from _____ _____ .

(e) When you can't think of a topic, _____ through the

_____ of a book in a subject you _____ .

(f) Once you've selected a topic, _____ _____ on it right away.

Check your responses in 5.

4————————————————

Now let's deal with some examples. Of the following topics, check which *one* you think is the best topic for a short paper.

1. The life of John Lennon   ☐ Go to **6**.
2. John Lennon and the Beatles   ☐ Go to **7**.
3. The use of imagery in John Lennon's song
   "God"   ☐ Go to **8**.
4. The use of imagery in John Lennon's songs   ☐ Go to **9**.

5————————————————

(a) Select a topic that is <u>interesting</u> to you, if possible.
(b) Select a topic your <u>instructor</u> is interested in.
(c) Select a topic that is <u>not too technical</u> and does not require <u>extensive research.</u>
(d) Select a topic from <u>daily experience.</u>
(e) When you can't think of a topic, <u>thumb</u> through the <u>index</u> of a book in a subject you <u>like.</u>
(f) Once you've selected a topic, <u>get started</u> on it right away.

If you answered all these correctly, go to **4**.
If you missed any of these items, reread Frame **3** again and make certain you know the correct responses. Then go to **4**.

6————————————————

No, let's think about this one. Remember, a short paper is only going to run a couple of pages in length. If a good topic for a short paper is an incident from a daily experience, how do you expect to write about the *life* of someone? Even if Lennon had been a midget, his life story would not be a good topic for a short paper. It would make a better long research paper.
  Go back to **4** and try another answer.

7————————————————

It's highly doubtful that in a short paper you could cover all of John Lennon's association with the Beatles. You would need to narrow the topic down more and it would mean a lot of research. It is too large a topic for a short paper.

Return to **4** and try another response.

8————————————————

Right. This topic is narrow enough for a short paper. You would carefully read the song and then select from "God" examples of the images he created. Then you would check to see if all the images are related to a particular theme or idea. Good selection.

Go to **10** and continue.

9————————————————

No. You'd be biting off more than you could chew in one paper. The topic is too broad because Lennon wrote many, many songs.

Return to **4** and try another answer. This time, think carefully.

10————————————————

L = List all your ideas related to the topic of the paper.

The second step to writing a short paper is to list on a piece of paper all the ideas you have about the topic. At this point you don't worry about the order of your ideas or whether you will even use them all in your final paper. What you are doing in this step is forcing yourself to jot down in writing whatever you know and think you can use in your paper that is related to the topic.

Here's an example of what a list of ideas might look like if you were going to write on the topic *What Makes a Good Driver*.

1. Drives at the proper speed for road conditions.
2. Checks brakes regularly.
3. Keeps tires in shape.
4. Obeys all driving laws.
5. Personal characteristics.
6. Doesn't drive when drinking.
7. Checks brakelights and directional lights regularly.
8. Changes oil regularly.
9. Doesn't tailgate other cars.

10. Doesn't drive when tired.
11. Doesn't drive when emotionally upset.

Notice that there is no order to this list. The items are just ideas that might occur in your head as you think through the topic. If you were comparing two things, such as a good driver versus a bad driver, you'd have two lists of ideas. The next step will be to order the ideas and eliminate ideas which don't belong. For instance, Item 8 above does not really have anything to do with actual driving (though some might argue that maintaining a safe vehicle is the mark of a good driver). But again, that is not important at this step. What is important is that you *do not* attempt to begin writing your paper until you first list ideas for possible use in the paper.

Now, turn to **11** and try a problem on your own.

11——————————————————

Let's pretend again. Suppose you are in an English composition class and your instructor says you have 45 minutes to write a short paper describing a penny, a coin you see almost daily. The trick is that you can't look at a penny while you are writing and must do it from memory. Make a list in the space below of all the things you could use to describe a penny. The first idea has been filled in for you as an example. Hey, put that penny back in your pocket!

1. Lincoln's head profile _____
2. _____
3. _____
4. _____
5. _____
6. _____
7. _____
8. _____
9. _____
10. _____
11. _____

Check your list against ours in **12**.

12————————————————————

Check your penny list with the following. They don't have to be in the same order.

1. Lincoln's head profile
2. Lincoln memorial or wheat stalks (depends on issue date)
3. In God We Trust
4. E Pluribus Unum
5. Liberty
6. United States of America
7. One cent
8. Mint mark or a letter code showing where minted
9. Date minted
10. Round, three-fourths of an inch in diameter
11. One-sixteenth of an inch thick

You may have other items listed such as a raised edge or a raised design, but these are the ones we'll use in later examples.

Even though a penny is a common coin, it is not necessarily easy to remember 10 items on a penny. But the thought process you used to list all the items you could remember is exactly the thought process necessary to writing a good paper. An essay is, after all, nothing more than your thoughts being presented to someone. Therefore, this second step is vital. *Never* attempt to just sit down and start writing. You'll waste too much time. *Think out your ideas first by listing them.*

To make certain you understand **Step L: List**, check the correct statement below:

1. Listing your ideas about a topic on a piece of
   paper before writing an essay is best.   ☐ Go to **13**.

2. Writing your ideas out in a rough draft is the
   best way to get started on an essay.   ☐ Go to **14**.

13————————————————————

Right you are. You understand this step. Go on to **15**.

CAN YOU SPELL 90% OF THESE WORDS? BET YOU CAN'T.

Have someone read these words to you, using them in a sentence. We bet you can't get 90% of them correct. Two points for each correct spelling.

1. stationery
2. February
3. scissors
4. niece
5. receive
6. foreign
7. chocolate
8. bicycle
9. appreciate
10. occasion
11. anxious
12. autumn
13. squirrel
14. calendar
15. especially
16. disease
17. governor
18. against
19. tobacco
20. sleigh
21. nickel
22. stomach
23. cousin
24. celebrate
25. chimney
26. naughty
27. whose
28. orchestra
29. psychology
30. acre
31. believe
32. castle
33. chose
34. desert
35. easily
36. either
37. whether
38. guard
39. neighbor
40. recess
41. quiet
42. scene
43. taught
44. thought
45. though
46. usually
47. valuable
48. Wednesday
49. wrist
50. antidisestablishmentarianism

14—————————————————

Nope. Something must have gotten lost in the translation, as they say. Listing is important because it forces you to *think first*, not write first. Thinking through the possible ideas about your topic *always* helps you collect your thoughts *before* attempting to write. Hopefully, you'll see why as you work through the rest of the steps in **SLOWER**.

Go to **15**.

15————————————————

O = Order your ideas.

Once you have thought through the possible ideas related to your topic and listed them on paper, you should order or **organize** them into a useful skeleton or outline from which you can begin writing. Grouping your ideas, then separating the general ideas from the examples, is what is meant by ordering. (This is treated in detail in Chapter 2, page 17. Refer to that chapter if you have problems here.) For instance, if you did have to write a paper on the topic "What Makes A Good Driver?," how would you **order** or organize the ideas listed in **10**? Look again at all the items listed in **10** and answer these questions.

1. Do any items need to be deleted from the list? ————

2. Which ones, if any? ————

3. Are there any items which seem to be the same type of things or related somehow? ————

4. Which ones, if any? ————

Check your answers in **16**.

16————————————————

Compare your answers with the following:

1. Yes.
2. Item 8. (Changing the oil has nothing to do with being a good driver. Checking brakes, tires, and brakelights has to do with safety, the concern of a good driver).
3. Yes.
4. Items 1, 4, 6, and 9 all deal with the act of driving itself. Items 2, 3, and 7 all deal with checking for safety features. Items 5, 10, and 11 deal with personal characteristics of the driver.

Basically, then, there are three general categories listed for what makes a good driver: (1) driving characteristics; (2) safety checks; and (3) personal characteristics. Plotted out, it might look like this:

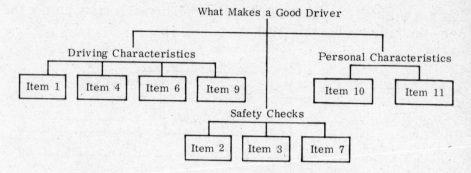

A more typical ordering might look something like this:

What Makes A Good Driver

I. Driving characteristics
   A. Drives at the proper speed for road conditions.
   B. Obeys all driving laws.
      1. Doesn't tailgate other cars.
      2. Doesn't drive when drinking.

II. Safety checks
   A. Checks brakes regularly.
   B. Checks brakelights and direction lights regularly.
   C. Keeps tires in shape.

III. Personal characteristics
   A. Doesn't drive when tired.
   B. Doesn't drive when emotionally upset.

The actual form or way you order your ideas is not important as long as the ideas are organized by their similar characteristics. Notice that under I.B in the outline above that two items have been listed under "Obeys all driving laws." This is because the two items are examples of driving laws which need to be obeyed. This, then, is what is meant by ordering your ideas.

To help clarify **Step O = Order** even more, go to **17** now.

17————————————————————

To make certain you understand the importance and procedure for **Step O = Order**, use the item numbers listed in **12** (the penny) and place them in the blanks below in the order you think they belong. If you can't remember which characteristics are on "heads" and which on "tails," take out a penny! (You probably listed other characteristics, but for the frames coming up, use our list.)

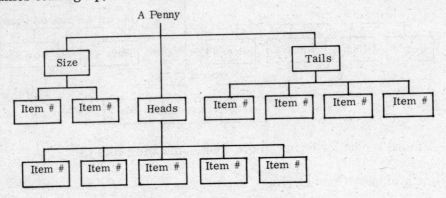

A Penny

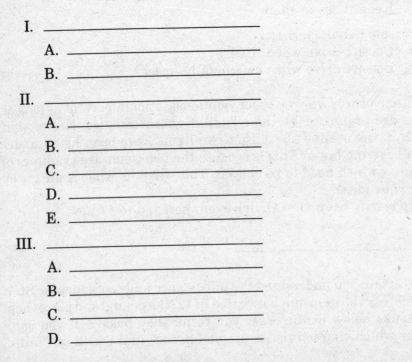

Check your answers in **19**.

18

Using the same items listed in **12**, fill in the blanks in the following organizational outline.

A Penny

I. _____

   A. _____

   B. _____

II. _____

   A. _____

   B. _____

   C. _____

   D. _____

   E. _____

III. _____

   A. _____

   B. _____

   C. _____

   D. _____

Check your answers in **20**.

19————————————————————

Under size, you should have Items 10 and 11. Under heads, you should have Items 1, 3, 5, 8, and 9. Under tails, you should have Items 2, 3, 4, 6, and 7. Notice that the idea behind **Step O = Order** is to logically put items together as a group. This will get your ideas organized so that when you start writing, they can be pulled together. But that's getting into the next step.

For now, go to **18**.

20————————————————————

Compare your answers with the following:

A Penny

 I. Size, or Shape, or Description of Size
   A. Round, 3/4ths in. in diameter
   B. 1/16 in. thick

 II. Heads
   A. Lincoln's head profile
   B. In God We Trust
   C. Liberty
   D. Mint mark
   E. Date minted

 III. Tails
   A. Lincoln memorial or wheat stalks
   B. E Pluribus Unum
   C. United States of America
   D. One cent

Notice that regardless of the form you use for ordering ideas about a penny that there are three general categories into which all items fit.

There are, of course, other ways to order your ideas about a penny. For instance, you could divide the items into two categories: (1) illustrations and (2) inscriptions. Such an ordering would look like this:

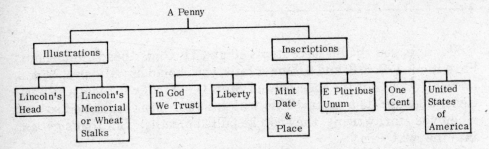

Which one of the three ways of ordering ideas is best depends entirely on you. The best way is the one that works best for you.
Go to **21**.

21————————————————

Check the response you think is correct.

The idea behind **Step O = Order** is to logically order all the ideas you have listed during Step 2 before you attempt to write your paper.

☐ True. Go to **23**.
☐ False. Go to **24**.

22————————————————

Put the ideas in steps **SLO** into practice. If you have a paper you must write for a class you are taking, use the steps to get you started. If you don't have a paper assigned to write, select your own topic. In either case, use the following space below to guide you through **SLO**.

Step 1. Select a topic: _____

Step 2. List your ideas: 1. _____

2. _____

3. _____

4. _____

5. _____

6. _____

7. _____

Step 3. **Organize** your ideas:

Naturally there is no answer key for your work. But you can check back over the frames to see if you have done the steps correctly. We'll come back to this work later.

Right now, go to **25**.

23————————————————

Good. You've got the picture.

Go to **22** for a practical application of the steps you've learned so far.

24————————————————

Whoops! We must have failed to get the main point about **Step O = Order** across. Well, if you didn't get it before, get it now. Ready? Here it is: The idea behind this third step is to logically order all the ideas you listed in Step 2 before you attempt to write your paper.

OK? Go back to **22**.

25————————————————

The fourth step in the **SLOWER** formula for better writing is **W** = **Write** a first draft. Few people can get by with just one draft or version of a paper. If you are writing in class during a timed period, your instructor is not going to expect you to write more than one draft. However, he will expect you to correct it, to draw lines indicating where you want a sentence or paragraph to be switched and to rephrase certain parts. But when you are writing outside of class, you have time (and you are expected to take the time) to write a second, third, or even fourth draft, if necessary. However, if you have done steps **SLO** carefully, you will probably not need to worry about a lot of rewriting, though there generally is always some rewriting necessary.

It is best to leave plenty of room for revision when you start writing from your list of ordered ideas. If you write it by hand, leave good, wide margins and write on every other line. If you type your first draft, again leave good-sized margins and double or triple space. This leaves room for making changes without getting things all crammed together.

Once you start turning your ideas into sentences and paragraphs, you may need to reorganize your ideas again. That's perfectly natural. But, hopefully, you will be reorganizing your ideas to fit the movement and flow of your paper as it begins to take shape.

This book does not have the space to cover everything that needs to be said about the actual writing of a paper. You either have taken or will take an English composition course at some time. That's where you have gotten or will get specific help in writing. But we can give you a few helpful guidelines for writing a first draft.

Go to **26**.

26————————————————

Remember the penny? Let's go back to it for a moment. In **18** you were asked to order items that would help you write a paper which describes a penny. Here is that ordered list again.

A Penny

    I. Size
        A. Three-fourths of an inch in diameter
        B. One-sixteenth of an inch thick

   II. One side (heads)
        A. Lincoln's profile
        B. In God We Trust
        C. Liberty
        D. Place minted
        E. Date minted

  III. Other side (tails)
        A. Lincoln Memorial
        B. E Pluribus Unum
        C. United States of America
        D. One Cent

Now, on the blank space that follows, write a short paper based on the ideas listed above. Feel free to change, add, or reorder the ideas. If you want to, look at a penny while you write.

WORDS OFTEN CONFUSED

Do you know the correct word to use? Fill in the blank with the letter of the correct word.

1. I liked it all _____ the last chapter.
   (a) accept   (b) except

2. He _____ the older part so that it fit the new one.
   (a) adopted   (b) adapted

3. Let's hope the medicine will have no _____ effect on her.
   (a) adverse   (b) averse

4. My _____ is not to _____ him on the matter.
   (a) advise   (b) advice

5. The story completely _____ him.
   (a) alluded   (b) eluded

6. I'm _____ to go.
   (a) all ready   (b) already

7. For years, he has _____ the guilt alone.
   (a) born   (b) borne

8. The new _____ building cost a fortune.
   (a) capital   (b) capitol

9. Upon this _____, I'll build my home.
   (a) cite   (b) sight   (c) site

10. The material felt very _____ to the touch.
    (a) course   (b) coarse

11. Why is _____ always served last?
    (a) dessert   (b) desert

12. She was _____ known as Mary Smythe before she wed.
    (a) formerly   (b) formally

13. If you want to go, _____ fine with me.
    (a) it's   (b) its

14. Use the _____ one mentioned in the list above.
    (a) latter   (b) later

15. The tie was _____ about his neck.
    (a) loose   (b) lose

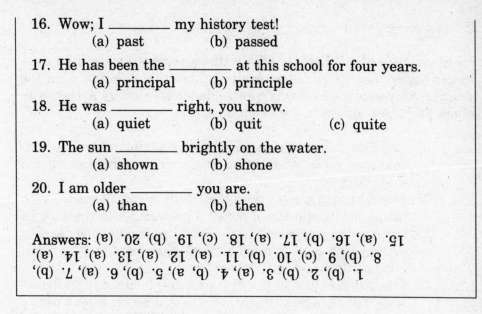

16. Wow; I _____ my history test!
    (a) past   (b) passed

17. He has been the _____ at this school for four years.
    (a) principal   (b) principle

18. He was _____ right, you know.
    (a) quiet   (b) quit   (c) quite

19. The sun _____ brightly on the water.
    (a) shown   (b) shone

20. I am older _____ you are.
    (a) than   (b) then

Answers: 15. (a), 16. (b), 17. (a), 18. (c), 19. (b), 20. (a),
8. (b), 9. (c), 10. (b), 11. (a), 12. (a), 13. (a), 14. (a),
1. (b), 2. (b), 3. (a), 4. (b, a), 5. (b), 6. (a), 7. (b),

27————————————————————

Compare the first draft you just wrote on the penny with the example below. Write down any comments you have about the example compared with your paper in the margin.

Description of a Penny

A penny, or 1 cent piece, is a round coin about three-quarters of an inch in diameter and about one-sixteenth of an inch thick. It is hard, made from the metals bronze and copper. It takes 100 pennies to make $1.

On one side of the coin, usually called "heads," there is a profile of President Abraham Lincoln's head. Above his head are the words "In God We Trust." On his left is the word "Liberty." On Lincoln's right appears the date the coin was minted and a letter under the date representing the place where it was minted.

On the other side of the penny, referred to as "tails," there is a picture of the Lincoln Memorial in Washington, D.C. Above the Memorial appear the words, "United States of America." Under that, in smaller letters, are the words, "E Pluribus Unum." Under the Memorial are the words "One Cent."

Your first draft should have the same basic three-paragraph organization as this sample paper does.

Go to **28** now.

28———————————————————

The fifth step in **SLOWER** is **E** = **Examine** for errors. Let's examine the sample paper. Your paper is naturally going to be different from the example, but notice the following points. Place a checkmark in the blank as you find these things in the sample paper.

_____ 1. The first paragraph has added such descriptive comments as "one cent piece" and "round coin" but uses the items listed under I in **26**.

_____ 2. The first paragraph also contains comments about the coin being hard and made of metal. This was not in the ordered list, but they do belong here. Don't be afraid to add ideas or items which come to mind as you write your own first draft. Did you do this in your paper?

_____ 3. The last sentence in the first paragraph does not really belong. The purpose of the paper was to _describe_ what a penny looks like, not to discuss its value. The last sentence in paragraph 1 needs to be omitted from a final draft.

_____ 4. The second paragraph deals only with one side of the coin. Does your first draft do this?

_____ 5. In the second paragraph, the place minted is mentioned last even though it appeared second from the last on the ordered list of ideas. The change is valid because the place minted appears under the date on a penny.

_____ 6. A new paragraph is started when discussion of the "tails" side begins. This is correct according to the way we outlined our ideas. Did you do it in your paper?

_____ 7. The order of items III.B and C are changed in the last paragraph, but it is correct to do so because the items are being described in order of appearance on the penny.

_____ 8. There are three major areas or categories in the list of ordered items and three paragraphs in the paper. This is correct. Does your paper contain three paragraphs based on the three categories in the list? It should.

Now go to **29**.

29————————————————————

Read aloud your first draft (in Frame **26**) about the penny. Examine it for the following things.

1. I have covered the topic carefully and properly enough for the assignment.
2. I have followed my organizational order and started new paragraphs when necessary.
3. The ideas or points in the paper move smoothly and easily from one to the other and are not all jumbled up.
4. Each sentence sounds clear and would make sense to someone else.
5. I have punctuated correctly (the right use of commas, apostrophes, colons, semicolons, etc.).
6. I have checked the dictionary for the spelling of all words I have doubts about.
7. My title reflects what the point of my paper is.

If you left good-sized margins and space between lines as you were directed earlier, you should have room to make your first draft corrections. When you have examined your first draft properly, all of the above statements in the checklist can be answered "yes."

Go to **30**.

30————————————————————

Way back in **22** you were asked to select a topic, list your ideas about the topic, and then order them. Now it's time to return to the work you did in that frame and put it to use. In the following space write a first draft based on the information you listed and organized in **22**. Feel free to reorganize before you start.

When you are finished, go to **31**.

EXAMINE YOUR PAPERS FOR THESE ERRORS

1. **Run-on or run-together sentences**. Do not run one sentence into the next with no punctuation separating them. End the first sentence with a period and begin the next sentence with a capital letter, or use a semicolon.

   Example: He enjoys watching them practice he thinks they are excellent players.
   Correction: He enjoys watching them practice. He thinks they are . . . etc.

2. **Comma splices**. Do not join or link two sentences with a comma.

   Example: Highway 101 is a very busy highway, thousands of trucks and cars use it everyday.
   Correction: Highway 101 is a very busy highway. Thousands of trucks and cars use it everyday.

3. **Fragment sentences**. Do not write partial or pieces of a sentence. Every sentence must have a subject and a verb. (Remember your English classes?) Usually fragments are parts of a sentence which should be attached to a complete sentence. While professional writers and advertisers can get away with using fragments, you can't as a student—not usually, anyway.

   Example: I do not have the prettiest teeth. As you can see.
   Correction: I do not have the prettiest teeth, as you can see.

4. **Shift in point of view**. Avoid shifting from one person (I, you, he, we, one) to another.

   Example: If one wishes to travel, you should save money.
   Correction: If one wishes to travel, one should save money.
         Or: If you wish to travel, you should save money.

5. **Dangling modifiers**. A dangling modifier is a phrase or part of a sentence which does not clearly or logically relate to another part of a sentence.

   Example: Looking out the window, an unusual sight caught my eye.
   Correction: Looking out the window, I saw an unusual sight. (The "I" is looking out the window, not the "unusual sight.")

31————————————————

Return to **29** and use the checklist for **Step E = Examine** for errors. If you cannot answer "yes" to all of these, change your first draft so that you can.

Go to **32** to get suggestions for the last step, **R = Revise**, into a final draft.

32————————————————

The last step in the **SLOWER** method is **R = Revise** your paper. You may have to revise more than once before you are satisfied with a final draft for handing in. Even expert writers like us have to revise several times before they get their final copy the way they want it. (You'll never guess how many times we rewrote this book!) That's why they are experts. They don't feel that every word they write is precious and needs to be saved. They are willing to write, rewrite, throw away, and write again.

As a student, you're not expected to be an expert writer. But there are some things instructors expect from you and there are some things you should do to impress your instructor that you are better than the average student. Here are some pointers to consider when revising your paper.

1. If you discover you need to **rearrange** things you have written or to add new paragraphs, use your scissors, or better yet, use a computer word processor, to cut up your first draft and reorder it the way you want it. (Don't waste time copying parts you are satisfied with.) Then you can see the paper in its final order, *before* you complete your final draft. If you misspelled a word, scratch through it and write the correct spelling above it or next to it.
2. If you do not type, make certain your **handwriting** is clear and that you have not written words over one another on your final draft. If you misspelled a word, scratch through it and write the correct spelling above it or next to it.
3. If you type your final draft, **proofread** it carefully. Don't be afraid to make changes with a pen if you notice mistakes. As long as your corrections are neatly made, your instructor will not consider your paper messy because you have marked on it. Typed papers should be double spaced.
4. **Number your pages** and make certain your name is on *all* pages of the final draft.

5. If you are writing a report or review of a book, play, movie, or something that has a title, do not use the book's title or play's title, etc., as your title. The **title** for your paper should be one you make up.

6. If you are **quoting** or using material from something you have read, be sure to put quotation marks around it and state the source. In the academic world it's "legal" to steal (or borrow) someone's ideas or quote what they say as long as you indicate where you stole it from.

7. Always **read your paper aloud**. It helps you hear what your paper sounds like and helps you spot errors you wouldn't see if you read silently. If possible get someone who is good in English or in the subject of your paper and have him or her read and comment on your paper.

Following these suggestions is no guarantee of a good grade, but following them will certainly improve your paper.

Go now to **33**.

33———————————————

Stand up and stretch, scratch, and yawn. Sit down, then go to **34**.

PUNCTUATION

Punctuation can make a difference. This sign

> PRIVATE
> NO SWIMMING
> ALLOWED

means something different from this one:

> PRIVATE?
> NO. SWIMMING
> ALLOWED.

Following are a few punctuation rules that may help you.

- Use commas in a list.   ". . . red, white, and blue."

- Enclose parenthetical expressions between commas.   "The student, who had been absent, completed the course."

- Use a comma before a conjunction introducing an independent clause.   "No writing was required, but the student continued to work with the tutor."

- Use a colon to introduce a list of particulars.   "The successful artist needs three things: time, talent, and discipline."

- Use a semicolon to separate main clauses not joined by one of the conjunctions and, but, or, nor, for, or main clauses joined by an adverb such as also, however, then, or thus.   "Never wait for inspiration; when it comes, let it find you hard at work."

  "The student spent many hours in class; however, she never studied at home."

For practice, add punctuation to each of the following sentences to get a different meaning.*

1. The escaping convict dropped a bullet in his leg.
2. The butler stood by the door and called the guests names as they arrived.
3. I am sorry you can not come with us.
4. Do not break your bread or roll in your soup.
5. The murderer protested his innocence an hour after he was put to death.

Answers:

1. The escaping convict dropped, a bullet in his leg.
2. The butler stood by the door and called the guest's names as they arrived.
3. I am sorry. You can not come with us.
4. Do not break your bread, or roll in your soup.
5. The murderer protested his innocence. An hour after, he was put to death.

*From Willard R. Espy, *Another Almanac of Words at Play.*

34———————————————————

Feel better? Good. Now use the suggestions listed in **32** to help you revise the paper you wrote in **30**. When you have finished, turn your final revision in to your instructor—and cross your fingers. If the paper turns out to be a bomb, ask your instructor for some suggestions on how to improve it. If nothing else, that will make your next paper for that class more successful.

If you had trouble so far or if you need some ideas or help for a composition class, then go to **P1** and do the following practice sessions. You will find them valuable.

If you feel you understand the process of writing short papers and had little difficulty with this section of the book, then you're finished. Take a vacation in Hawaii. If you need a brush up later, try going to **P1**.

Chapter Five Practice Exercises

P1———————————————————

Which of the following topics would be best for a short paper of about two pages in length? Check one.

(a) How to Fry Chicken   ☐ Go to **P2**.
(b) How to Build a House   ☐ Go to **P3**.
(c) How to Manage a Motel   ☐ Go to **P4**.
(d) How to Get to the Moon on Foot   ☐ Go to **P33**.

P2———————————————————

Sure. Of the four topics mentioned, frying chicken would not need the coverage the other three topics would. Good thinking.
Go to **P5**.

P3———————————————————

Maybe you could do a two-page paper on building a house, but would it really tell somebody who wanted to build a house *how* to do it? Could a short paper cover construction, plumbing, electricity, gas, etc.? It's doubtful.
Look for another response in **P1**.

P4————————————————————

If you can write a two-page paper on this topic that is any good, you could probably get it published. However, we doubt that it can be done.

Look again at **P1** and select another answer.

P5————————————————————

Which of the following topics would be best for a short paper of about two pages or less? Check one.

(a) Television Advertising	☐	Go to **P6**.
(b) My Favorite TV Ad	☐	Go to **P7**.
(c) Television's Top 20 Advertisers	☐	Go to **P8**.

P6————————————————————

You'd be better off not to try. The topic is too big and needs to be narrowed down to some smaller aspect of TV advertising.

Try another response in **P5**.

P7————————————————————

Right. It's a very small topic—one ad—and all you need to do is explain why it is your favorite ad. Good choice.

Go to **P9**.

P8————————————————————

Nope. It's too big for a small paper. You might handle *one* of TV's big advertisers but not all twenty.

Try a response in **P5** that looks less complicated.

P9————————————————————

Which of the following topics would make a good topic for a short (two-page), descriptive essay? Check one.

(a) Your School Campus   ☐ Go to **P10**.
(b) The California Coast Line   ☐ Go to **P11**.
(c) Your Bedroom   ☐ Go to **P12**.

P10————————————

If you have a small campus, you might be able to write a short descriptive essay. It's possible; however, of the three choices (c), describing your bedroom, seems the easiest task. But then if you sleep in a phone booth, you'll have to write about the campus.
   Go on to **P13**.

P11————————————

No way! The California coastline is long and as varied as can be. Books have been written to describe it, so it's doubtful you can do it in a short paper.
   Try **P9** again.

P12————————————

Yes. Of the three, this is the narrowest topic in scope. Short papers are not intended to get you involved in large-scale topics. Good selection.
   Go to **P13**.

P13————————————

Pretend you're in an English composition class and your instructor tells you to write about the advantages of eating at a McDonald's. In the blanks below, list some reasons you might include in writing your paper.

Advantages

1. _____
2. _____
3. _____
4. _____
5. _____

6. _____

7. _____

8. _____

9. _____

10. _____

Compare your list with the examples in **P14**.

P14——————————————————

You may have a list which is somewhat different in wording, but check to see how many ideas here are similar to yours.

1. Don't have to dress up
2. Food is cheaper than most restaurants
3. Convenient
4. Speed of service
5. Good assortment of food
6. Hamburger, french fries, and milk shake are nutritious
7. Good place to meet friends
8. Plenty of parking space

That's all we can think of right now. Maybe you got 10 items. Good for you if you did. (No, we don't own stock in McDonald's.)
   Go to **P15**.

P15——————————————————

Use the numbers of the items listed in **P14** and order them in a way that would help you write a first draft from your ordered list. Use the space below.

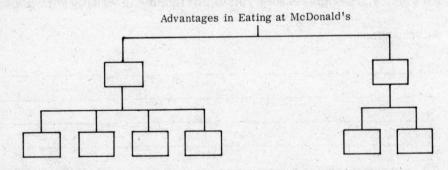

Advantages in Eating at McDonald's

Go to **P16**.

P16————————————————————

Pause here to eat your hamburger. Don't throw the wrapper on the floor. Then go to **P17**.

P17————————————————————

Compare your answers in **P15** with the following:

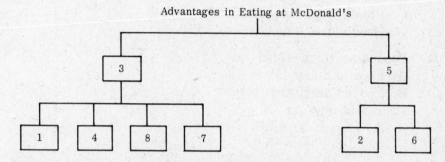

Advantages in Eating at McDonald's

It's possible that your answers are different but still acceptable. This ordering breaks the list of items into two major groups: conveniences and food assortment. Conveniences are that you don't have to dress (1), you get speedy service (4), there's plenty of parking space (8), and it's a good place to meet friends (7). We put 8 before 7 because it is a service of the establishment, whereas 7 is not the result of anything the business offers. The two items under food assortment are that the food is cheap (2) and nutritious (6). That's our reasoning. What's yours?
Go to **P18**.

P18————————————————————

Use the list in **P14** and the explanation in **P17** and make an outline you might use to write your paper.

Now go to **P19**.

P19————————————————

Compare your outline with the following:

Advantages

  I. Convenient (3)
     A. Don't have to dress up (1)
     B. Speed of service (4)
     C. Plenty of parking space (8)
     D. Good place to meet friends (7)

 II. Food Assortment Good (5)
     A. Food is cheap (2)
     B. Food is nutritious (6)
       1. Hamburger (6)
       2. French fries (6)
       3. Milk shake (6)

If this outline is not clear, go back to **P17** and read the explanation again or go to Chapter 2 for detailed help in organizing concepts.
If you understand this outline, go to **P20**.

P20————————————————

The objects listed below need to be organized into common groups. Decide which items belong in which group. List the objects under the proper group.

Items	Group 1	Group 2	Group 3
Pencil			
Fork			
Screwdriver			
Cup			
Wrench			
Plate			
Knife			
Shovel			
Ink pen			

Check your answers in **P22**.

P21———————————————

Now that you have organized the items into groups, write in the blanks below a word or phrase which you feel could serve as headings for each group and a title for all three groups.

Title for all three groups: _____

Heading for Group 1: _____

Heading for Group 2: _____

Heading for Group 3: _____

Check your answers in **P23**.

P22———————————————

Group 1:   Fork, cup, plate, knife
Group 2:   Screwdriver, wrench, shovel
Group 3:   Pencil, ink pen

If you were correct, go back to **P21**.
If you missed any, go back to **P20** and fill in the blanks correctly. Notice why they are grouped as they are.
Then go to **P21**.

P23———————————————

Title for all groups: Utensils, tools, or implements used by man
Title for Group 1:   Eating utensils, or kitchen utensils
Title for Group 2:   Work utensils
Title for Group 3:   Writing utensils, or tools

Your wording may differ, but you should have the same basic ideas. Go to **P24**.

P24———————————————

Using the list of items in **P20** and the headings in **P23**, fill out the following outline.

I.   Title _____
       A. _____
            1. _____
            2. _____
            3. _____
            4. _____
       B. _____
            1. _____
            2. _____
            3. _____
       C. _____
            1. _____
            2. _____

Check your responses in **P27**.

P25——————————————————

We hope you are aware that these exercises are taking you through the first three steps of the **SLOWER** method for better writing. As a spot check, fill in the blanks below:

S = _____

L = _____

O = _____

Check your responses in **P28**.

P26——————————————————

Another suppose. Suppose you have to write a short paper on your favorite magazine. Fill in the following spaces:

S   What is your favorite magazine? _____

L   List some reasons why it is.

    1. _____

    2. _____

    3. _____

    4. _____

    5. _____

    6. _____

O   Arrange your reasons in the order you would use them in your paper. Use the numbers above.

    _____

    _____

    _____

    _____

    _____

    _____

Can you place into groups any of the reasons above? If you can, do so in the following space:

Go to **P29**.

P27

  I.   Title: Some Implements Used By Man
     A. Eating utensils
        1. Fork
        2. Knife
        3. Plate
        4. Cup
     B. Work utensils
        1. Screwdriver
        2. Wrench
        3. Shovel
     C. Writing utensils
        1. Pencil
        2. Ink pen

What you now have is a working outline of ordered ideas you could use to write a first draft on "Some Implements Used By Man." Save it. It may be useful someday.

Go back to **P25**.

P28

S = **Select** a topic
L = **List** your ideas about that topic
O = **Order** your list of ideas

If you were correct, go back to **P26**.

If you missed any of these, study this frame until you have it memorized.

Then go back to **P26**.

P29

By now you should know the first three steps of the **SLOWER** formula. Fill in the following blanks for the last three steps.

W = _____

E = _____

R = _____

Check your responses in **P31**.

P30————————————————

As you were told earlier in this section, this book does not have the space and is not intended to teach you how to write individual sentences or paragraphs within your papers. But we have shown you how to select topics, how to order your ideas, and some procedures for putting together an orderly paper so that it will stand a better chance of surviving an instructor's red pen.

We hope you realize that you also have some outlines which are now ordered and ready for use in writing a first draft (description of a penny, characteristics of a good driver, eating at McDonald's, favorite magazine). Use them if you are taking an English composition class or whenever they fit an assignment. At least *use* the **SLOWER** formula the next time you have to write. You'll get results.

- If you are a super student, go to **P32**.
- If you are a "get-by" student, go to the next chapter of the book. You're through here.

P31————————————————

W = **Write** a first draft
E = **Examine** your draft for errors
R = **Revise** your draft into a final one

If you were correct, go to **P30**.
If you missed any, study this frame. Then go to **P30**.

P32————————————————

Hi, super student. Here's a good idea for you. Use the **WER** steps from **SLOWER** on one or all of the ordered lists you just completed in the previous frames. Submit the finished product to an instructor or burn it if you'd rather. But at least you've applied the **SLOWER** formula. And applying what you learn is what it's all about.

'Bye now.

P33——————————————

Forget it! You can't get there from here.
Walk back to **1**. Vooooomm.

CHAPTER SIX
Researching a Term Paper

GOALS AND OBJECTIVES

General Goals   When you complete this unit, you will

1. Have increased confidence in your ability to use the library
2. Use library resources when assigned research or term papers
3. Have increased confidence in your ability to write research papers
4. Apply the **SLOWER** formula to writing research papers

Specific Objectives   When you complete this unit, you will be able to

1. Locate and use correctly the following library resources in your campus library:

   (a)   Card catalog
   (b)   *The Reader's Guide to Periodical Literature*
   (c)   Open and closed stacks
   (d)   *Dictionary of American Biography*
   (e)   *Dictionary of Modern English Usage*
   (f)   Periodical collection
   (g)   *Encyclopedia Brittanica*
   (h)   *Who's Who*
   (i)   The librarian

2. Distinguish between the Dewey Decimal and Library of Congress classification systems.
3. Locate specific information on the mechanics and format used in research papers.

Check any of the following items you are *not* familiar with:

☐   1. The card catalog
☐   2. *The Reader's Guide to Periodical Literature*

☐   3. Open stacks and closed stacks
☐   4. Dewey Decimal Classification
☐   5. Library of Congress Classification
☐   6. *Dictionary of American Biography*
☐   7. Abstracts
☐   8. *A Dictionary of Modern English Usage*
☐   9. Call number
☐ 10. Periodical room

If you checked more than six of the above, then you are in the right place. Go to **1**.

If you checked six or fewer of the above, go to **1**, too! We just used the checklist to get your mind on the subject of research and the term paper.

1————————————————

The first thing we want you to do is to make certain you know your school library. The only way to do that is to actually go to your library. So . . . go to your library; *but bring us with you.*

Once you're inside the door, go to **2**.

2————————————————

You should be at the door of the library on your campus. If you aren't, you're lost. Somehow, get found.

Now, here's what you do. Go in and find the card catalog. The card catalog in your library may be a set of drawers containing cards for every book in that library, or it may be that your school's library has converted to microfilm or computer. Some libraries put the card catalog listings on microfilm to save space. If this is the case, look for a microfilm machine (it looks like a TV screen).

Every library is a bit different. If the card catalog for your library is on microfilm, it may contain listings of books in other libraries in the vicinity. Ask your librarian how it works. If you don't know where it is, ask one of the librarians. All librarians love to tell people about their library so don't be bashful.

Once you find the card catalog, go to **3**.

3————————————————

The card catalog is the foundation of the library. It contains a card or a microfilm listing for every book in the library. (Actually, it sometimes contains three cards or listings for every book because books are cataloged in three ways: by **author**, by **title**, and by **subject**. More about this later.) These cards are arranged alphabetically.

Use the card catalog and find a listing for the 1978 edition of a book entitled *The Population Bomb*. (Be certain you look in the "P" section. Titles beginning with *"the," "a,"* or *"an"* are listed under the second word.) When you find it, write the author's name here:

_____

Go to 5.

If your library doesn't have it, go ask the librarian to order it. Then go to 5.

4———————————————————————

There's no use figuring out where you're going to be later on; you may not be there at all. So the sensible thing is to do the very best you can all the time.

Robert F. Kennedy

You're supposed to be in 5.

5———————————————————————

If you found the right card, you know that the author is Paul R. Ehrlich. The entry for the 1978 edition (there are two editions listed prior to this one) should look something like this:

304.6V	Ehrlich, Paul R.
E33P-p	The population bomb/rev. ed. by Paul R. Ehrlich.
	New York, Ballantine Books 1978
	226 p. (A Sierra Club-Ballantine book)
	$9.95
	Bibliographical references included in "Footnotes" (p. 221–224) Bibliography: p. 225–226
	1. Population I. Title
	HB875.E35 301.3'2 68–6116

Notice the number in the upper left hand corner. This is what's known as a "call number" and it is your guide for finding the book in the library. The number on the card here and the one you are looking at in your library may be different. The numbering on the card here in the book is from a system known as the *Dewey Decimal Classification*.

Notice the number in the lower left hand corner of the card above. That number is also a "call number"; that one is based on the *Library of Congress Classification* system. If that is the number printed in the upper left hand corner of the card in your library, your library uses the Library of Congress system.

Go to **6**.

6————————————

A library uses one of two systems for classifying its book collection. What are the names of those two classification systems? Fill in the blanks.

(a) ————————————————————

(b) ————————————————————

Go to **8**.

7————————————

Which system does your library use? Fill in the blank.

————————————————————

Go to **9**.

8————————————

Check your answers with these:

(a) Library of Congress Classification
(b) Dewey Decimal Classification

Go to **7**.

9———————————————————— .

While you are still in the card catalog, notice all the information provided on the card or screen. Here's the listing for the first edition of *The Population Bomb*. Notice the difference between the 1968 edition and the 1978 one.

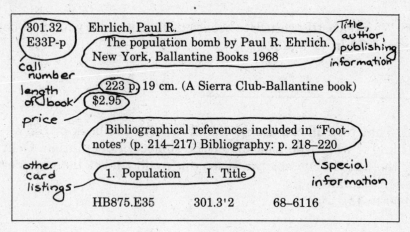

Go to **10**.

10————————————————————

Now go look under Ehrlich, Paul R. in the card catalog and see if you can find a card for *The Population Bomb* listed under the author's name.

If you do find one, go to **11**.

If you don't, make certain the librarian orders the book before you go to **12**.

11————————————————————

Now go look under Population in the card catalog and see if you can find a card for Ehrlich's book. (If your library doesn't have *The Population Bomb,* look under "Population" anyway to see what other books it does have on the subject.)

Then go to **12**.

12————————————————————

What is the point of having you look under three different listings for the same card? Check one.

(a) To keep you busy   ☐ Go to **13**.
(b) To show you that books are listed by author,
      title, and subject   ☐ Go to **14**.

13—————————————————

NAW. We have better things to keep you busy. Besides you know better.
   Go read (b) in **12** again.

14—————————————————

Right. That way, if you are not familiar with the book or the author,
you'll find it when you look under the subject of population. Or if you
knew the author but not the title, you could find it listed under the
author's last name.
   Go on to **15**.

15—————————————————

Sometimes, when looking in the **card catalog** under a special subject—
such as "population"—you'll see cards similar to this:

Population

   For further material on the above subject, consult the
SPECIAL COLLECTIONS which are checked below:
   (If you cannot find what you want, the librarian will
be glad to help you.)

☒ Pamphlet file   ☐ Public documents
☐ Clipping file   ☐ Picture collection
☐ Periodical indexes   ☐ Art collection
☐ Local history collection   ☐ Music collection
☐ Maps   ☐ Lantern slides

   What the librarian is trying to tell you is that there are other things
besides books about the subject. So, if you were doing research on the
subject of the population explosion, you could get additional information
in the pamphlet file. These resources are often more up to date than
books on the subject and should be considered.
   Go on to **16**.

16———————————————————

Libraries generally have an "open stacks" collection of books and sometimes "closed stacks" as well. Open stacks means that you can walk around among the shelves (stacks of books) and browse through them. "Closed stacks" means that you cannot browse or get a book yourself, but must present the call number of the book you want to the librarian and he or she will get it for you.

If you can browse around the stacks of books in your school library (open stacks), go to **17**.

If you have to present a call slip to a librarian to get most books (closed stacks), go to **18**.

17———————————————————

Use the call number on the card for Paul Ehrlich's *The Population Bomb* and go find the book. Look on the walls or book shelves for call numbers. Don't be afraid to ask the librarian for help if you get lost.

When you find the book, go to **19**.

18———————————————————

If you have never checked a book out of your library before, make out a call slip for Ehrlich's book, *The Population Bomb,* and check it out. It's a popular book and may already be checked out; but go through the check-out procedure anyway.

Then go to **20**.

19———————————————————

If you can't find the book, it may be checked out. That's OK. Look around that same general area. Notice that the books all deal with the same general subject. That's what the call numbers are all about. They group books of the same type together.

If you found the book, take it to the check-out desk. If you have never checked a book out of the library before, you need the experience. You can always turn the book back in before you leave the library. You need that experience, too!

Go to **20**.

20————————————————————————

Next on your little tour of the library will be the *Reader's Guide to Periodical Literature.* This index, unlike the card catalog, gives you titles of individual articles which appear in such periodicals as *Time, Fortune, New Republic, Saturday Review, Atlantic,* and many other magazines. Here is a sample entry from the *Reader's Guide** with an explanation of the listings.

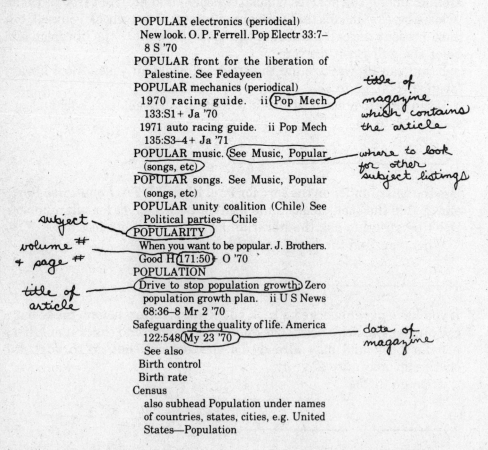

POPULAR electronics (periodical)
  New look. O. P. Ferrell. Pop Electr 33:7–
  8 S '70
POPULAR front for the liberation of
  Palestine. See Fedayeen
POPULAR mechanics (periodical)
  1970 racing guide. ii Pop Mech
  133:S1+ Ja '70
  1971 auto racing guide. ii Pop Mech
  135:S3–4+ Ja '71
POPULAR music. See Music, Popular
  (songs, etc)
POPULAR songs. See Music, Popular
  (songs, etc)
POPULAR unity coalition (Chile) See
  Political parties—Chile
POPULARITY
  When you want to be popular. J. Brothers.
  Good H 171:50+ O '70
POPULATION
  Drive to stop population growth. Zero
  population growth plan. ii U S News
  68:36–8 Mr 2 '70
  Safeguarding the quality of life. America
  122:548 My 23 '70
    See also
  Birth control
  Birth rate
Census
    also subhead Population under names
    of countries, states, cities, e.g. United
    States—Population

Handwritten annotations: title of magazine which contains the article; where to look for other subject listings; subject; volume # + page #; title of article; date of magazine

*Material from the Readers' Guide to Periodical Literature used in this textbook is reproduced by permission of The H. W. Wilson Company.

At the beginning of the *Reader's Guide* is a section which describes how to use it. There you will find a list of periodical titles explaining what "Pop Mech" stands for, or "Good H." We don't have room to describe in detail how to use the *Guide,* but you can always refer to the front section of it with your questions. And remember, librarians will be glad to help you.

For now, study carefully the sample entry from the *Reader's Guide.* Then go to **21**.

21————————————————————

Wherever you are now (you should still be in the library), go find the *Reader's Guide to Periodical Literature.* (It is usually in a general reference section.) When you find where the *Reader's Guide* is located, you will notice there are several very heavy volumes, all covering certain dates. Find the volume dated March 1970 to February 1971.

When you find it, go to **22**.

22————————————————————

You should have the *Reader's Guide* for March 1970 to February 1971. Check to make sure.

Good. Now look up the subject of population. Find the first page that deals with population.

Write the page number in the blank: ———— .

Go to **23**.

23————————————————————

If you are in the right place, you should have written Page 953 in the blank. (If you have any other page number you are in the wrong place or the wrong volume.) Now skim down the entries under *population* on Page 953 and find the listing for an article titled "Population Overgrowth, The Fertile Curse" written by the same man who wrote *The Population Bomb,* Paul R. Ehrlich. (Remember the card catalog entry?) Write the information requested in the blanks below:

(a) Title of magazine: ——————————————————————

(b) Page number: ————————

(c) Date of magazine: ——————————————

Check your answers in **25**.

24————————————

Now find the answers to the following questions.

(a) How many articles listed under population mention Paul Ehrlich?

_____

(b) How many of these entries are articles written by Ehrlich? _____

_____

(c) What are the other listings with his name but *not* written by him?

_____

Check your answers in **26**.

25————————————

Your answers should read:

(a) *Field and Stream*
(b) 58 (the + means the article is continued on other pages throughout the magazine)
(c) June 1970

Abbreviations used, remember, are all explained in the front of the *Reader's Guide* volume.
Go to **24**.

26————————————

Your answers should read:

(a) Five (if you said four, you probably forgot to turn the page to 954 for continued listings)
(b) Three, one of which is co-authored with J. P. Holden
(c) Interviews with him written by other people

Now go to **27**.

27————————————

Find the entry for the article "Hidden Effects of Overpopulation" and write in the information requested:

Name of magazine: _____

Date of issue: _____

Page number: _____

Authors: _____

Go to **28** when you are finished.

28————————————————

Check your answers with these:

Saturday Review
August 1, 1970
Page 52
Ehrlich and Holden

Now put the *Reader's Guide* you have been using back where it belongs. While you are in this area of your library, look around at the other types of index your library has. Check among the following the ones you see.

☐ *The Business Periodicals Index*. Specialized for those in business.
☐ *Social Sciences and Humanities Index* (formerly titled *International Index of Periodicals*). This one contains entries regarding articles appearing in scholarly journals—particularly in the humanities, arts, and social sciences.
☐ *New York Times Index*. Indexes the New York Times.
☐ *Engineering Index*. Specialized for the engineering field.
☐ *Education Index*. Specialized for those in education.

☐ Others: _____

_____

Good. Remember these works when you have a research paper to do. Go to **29**.

29————————————————

The card catalog is most useful in helping you locate books in the library, and the *Reader's Guide to Periodical Literature* is most useful in helping you locate current articles in popular magazines.

Check one: • True   ☐   Go to **31**.
                • False ☐   Go to **32**.

IF YOU HAVE A SCIENCE RESEARCH REPORT, these references may come in handy. Are you familiar with any of them?

American Scientist　　　　　　*Van Nostrand Scientific*
American Naturalist　　　　　　　*Encyclopedia*
American Zoologist　　　　　　*Physics Teacher*
Audobon Magazine　　　　　　*Sea Frontiers*
Bioscience　　　　　　　　　　*Science*
Ecology　　　　　　　　　　　*Scientific American*
Journal of Ecology　　　　　　*Undersea Technology*
McGraw-Hill Encyclopedia of
　Science and Technology

30————————————————

It's time to move on, this time to the periodical room (the place where they keep magazines). Using the information you wrote down in **27**, go to the periodicals and find the article by Ehrlich and Holden. Ask your librarian for help if you need it.

When you have located it, go to **33**.

31————————————————

You're right with us. Good thinking. Go to **30** now.

32————————————————

Either you goofed or we're doing a lousy job of teaching you. The statement is true. Reread it and try to figure out why you said *False*.

Ask your librarian if you don't believe us. Then go to **30**.

33————————————————

How did it go? Libraries vary so you may not have been able to find the issue of the magazine without help. In some libraries, periodicals are kept in bound editions out in open stacks. In other libraries, the closed stack method is used and magazines must be checked out just as books do. In either case, the most current issues of magazines are usually kept separately for easy access.

Go to **34**.

34 ——————————————————————

We've been keeping you pretty busy. Take a rest now and find a place to sit down and read the article you just located by Ehrlich and Holden. If the article doesn't look interesting, return the magazine (we just wanted you to see the article really was where the *Reader's Guide* said it would be) and look around for a magazine that does look interesting.

When you are all rested, go to **35**.

35 ——————————————————————

- If you are a "super" student, go to **36**.
- If you are a "get-by" student, go to **37**.

36 ——————————————————————

Now that we have you in the vicinity of the periodicals and journals, roam around or look over the list of periodicals which your library will have posted somewhere. Fill in the blanks below with at least six journals you never heard of before. Try to list one from six different areas, such as literature or history or science.

Unfamiliar journals:

1. _____

2. _____

3. _____

4. _____

5. _____

6. _____

Now pick one or two that look interesting, obtain recent copies and look them over. Amazing, isn't it, how much exists which we know nothing about? Sometime in your college career or future, these journals may be helpful to you.

Go to **37**.

37——————————————————

One more stop now. Go find the place in the library where the reference works are kept. Reference works are such things as encyclopedias, abstracts, yearbooks, dictionaries, atlases, and the like. When you get there, check which references your library has.

☐ *Encyclopedia Americana*
☐ *Encyclopedia Britannica*
☐ *McGraw-Hill Encyclopedia of Science*
☐ *International Encyclopedia of the Social Sciences*
☐ *The American Annual* (supplement to *Encyclopedia Americana*)
☐ *Brittanica Book of the Year* (supplement to *Encyclopedia Brittanica*)
☐ *World Almanac and Book of Facts*
☐ *United States Statistical Abstracts*
☐ *Webster's New International Dictionary*
☐ *Oxford English Dictionary*
☐ *Dictionary of American Biography*
☐ *Who's Who*
☐ A World Atlas

Most libraries have all of these in their collection. If you can't find one of them, ask your librarian where it is. Remember these references the next time you have a research paper to write.

Now go to **38**.

38——————————————————

Either on your own, or with the help of a librarian's assistant, check the following items as you find them in your library. (Not every library will have all of these.)

☐ Open stacks
☐ Closed stacks
☐ Typing rooms
☐ Duplicating machine for copying pages from books and
   journals
☐ Coeducational restrooms
☐ Reading rooms
☐ Study rooms
☐ Fire escapes
☐ Branches of the library in other buildings

☐ Microfilm readers
☐ Your librarian's name _____
☐ Good looking librarians
☐ Other: _____

Well, by now you should know your library a little better than before. Just remember this: Of all the aids in the library, the best one is your librarian or librarian's assistant. If you can't find what you need, ask for help. You'll get it.

Go to **39**.

39————————————

The point of familiarizing you with your own campus library is obvious. The resources there are no good to you unless you know what exists and where to find what you need. Many courses you take will require term papers or research papers on certain subjects. Half the battle in preparing a term paper is knowing where to look.

Suppose you are taking a sociology class and you are assigned a research paper on the topic of overpopulation. Order the items below in the way you would do them:

1. _____	(a)	Research reading.
2. _____	(b)	Write a rough draft.
3. _____	(c)	Collect research information.
4. _____	(d)	Make an outline or order ideas.
5. _____	(e)	Make bibliographic notecards.
6. _____	(f)	Rewrite final draft with a bibliography.
7. _____	(g)	Examine for errors and proper documentation.
8. _____	(h)	Narrow your topic.

Check your answers in **40**.

40————————————

Hopefully you used the basic ideas from the **SLOWER** formula to make your responses. Here's the order we suggest.

1. __(h)__ Narrow your topic; make certain you can cover your topic.

2. __(c)__   Collect research information; use the references we've already covered in the last frames.

3. __(a)__   Research reading; read what you found available.

4. __(e)__   Make bibliographic notecards for each reference you read. These cards will be discussed later.

5. __(d)__   Order your ideas or make an outline based on your notecards.

6. __(b)__   Write a rough draft from your outline or ordered list.

7. __(g)__   Examine your rough draft for errors and proper documentation.

8. __(f)__   Rewrite your final draft; include a bibliography.

If you had these ordered differently, note the order we suggest.

Note also the similarity to the **SLOWER** formula. The basic approach is the same.

Go to **41**.

41————————————————

Let's go back to your research topic: overpopulation. That's a pretty broad topic. You need to narrow it down. Which of the following is the narrowest topic? Check one.

- Overpopulation: The World's Problem   ☐
- One Effect of Overpopulation in Bill's Place, Pa.   ☐
- The Major Effects of Overpopulation in Southeast Asia ☐

Check your response in **42**.

42————————————————

We think the best choice of the three would be "One Effect of Overpopulation in Bill's Place, Pa." The other two topics cover too much territory even for a research paper. However, a good writer can creatively handle almost any writing assignment. The first consideration should be what your instructor wants in a research paper.

Now go to **43**.

43————————————————

Now that you have your topic narrowed down, which of the following would you do next? Check one.

- Look under "population" in the card catalog ☐
- Look under "overpopulation" in an encyclopedia ☐

Go to **44**.

44————————————————————

Your best bet would be to look under "population" in the card catalog.
Write down the call numbers of any books that seem to have anything to
do with the population explosion. If you see any cards which list *Special
Collections,* be certain to note where you should look.

Once you have found some possible books on the subject, which of the
following would you do next? Check one.

- Go find the books using the call numbers. ☐
- Go to the *Reader's Guide* and look under "population." ☐

Check your response in **45**.

45————————————————————

You could go get the books, but you'd be better off going to the *Reader's
Guide* or other sources first. Remember, what you are doing is gathering
information for possible resources. This way you will know how much
material is available before you get too far along. If there is not enough
material available, you may have to change topics.

Once you have located and collected all the information from all the
different sources, which of the following would you do next? Check one.

- Read from your reading material. ☐
- Make bibliographic notecards. ☐

Go to **46**.

46————————————————————

Actually, it would be a good idea to do both at the same time. About the
only "new" concept we've thrown at you here is the **bibliographic
notecard**.

Some instructors may require two kinds of research cards: one, the
bibliography card for a book or article on the subject being researched;

the other, a **notecard** containing information from the readings from the sources. Our recommendation is to combine the two types.

Using a 5 × 8 card for each book or article, put all the bibliographical information at the top of the card. (An acceptable order for listing a book and an article from a journal or magazine will be presented in another frame.) You should check with your instructor or librarian to see what form or style for listing resources is required. Some colleges have their own **style sheet** that all students are supposed to use. Find out before you begin making bibliography cards.

Usually there is room on the bibliography card to write some notes or quotes from the source you are reading. When you need more space, simply list the author's name or the title of the work at the top of a second card and write in the number 2. Do this with each additional card. Don't write on the back of a card. It is easier to work from note cards when you can place them in numerical order and don't have to turn them over. If you do a good job on your notecards, that is, keeping page references for exact words that you quote from the source material, or jotting down facts and figures you can use later in your research paper, you don't need to return to the library later for information you forgot or page numbers you didn't record.

Some people prefer to use a spiral notebook instead of cards because there is more room to take lengthy notes. Later, the pages can be torn out and ordered for the writing of a rough draft. Use what you prefer, but be sure to keep notes on all the reading sources you use.

These cards are extremely important when doing research and should contain all the information you are going to need to make footnotes and a bibliography (alphabetical list of books used in researching your paper) for your research paper.

On the following page is a sample bibliographic notecard for a book using a 5 × 8 card.

```
304.6V
E33P-p

Ehrlich, Paul R. The Population Bomb, rev.
     New York: Ballantine Books, 1968.


Ehrlich says in Chapter Two on pages
75-77 that...
```

(whatever you need to remember or whatever you think
about while reading the book which is important
for your paper.)

Notice that the call number is on the card in case you need to locate the book again at a later date when you are revising your paper. Notice, too, that all the information which will be needed in your bibliography is on the card:

1. Author (last name first)
2. Title (underlined)
3. Place of publication
4. Publisher
5. Date of publication

Always make certain your notecards contain this information.
Go to **47**.

47——————————————————

Here is an entry from *Reader's Guide* you should be familiar with by now.

> Hidden effects of overpopulation. P. R. Ehrlich and
> J. P. Holden. Sat. R. 53:52 Ag 1 '70

How would you list this information on a bibliographic notecard? Use the space below:

Compare your response with **48**.

48——————————————————

It should look something like this:

Ehrlich, P. R. and J. P. Holden, "Hidden Effects of Overpopulation," *Saturday Review,* Vol. 53 (August 1, 1970). p. 52.

Notice the difference between the way a book is listed and the magazine listing above:

1. Author, last name first (if more than one author is cited, the first one listed gets last name first; the others appear as shown above)

2. Title of article (with quotation marks around it)
3. Title of magazine (underlined)
4. Volume number of magazine, if available
5. Date of magazine (in parentheses)
6. Page number (p. for single page, pp. for more than one page)

If you don't know the proper order or your answer doesn't match this one, at least you should have *all* the information listed above. We'll discuss proper bibliographical order in a later frame.

Go to **49.**

SOCIAL SCIENCE JOURNALS: DO YOU KNOW THEM?

History Journals

American Historical Review (Quarterly)
Current History (Monthly)
History Today (Monthly)
Journal of American History (Quarterly)
Negro History Bulletin (Monthly—School year)

Sociology Journals

American Journal of Sociology (Bimonthly)
The American Sociology Review (Bimonthly)
Social Problems (Quarterly)
Social Science Quarterly
Social Research (Quarterly)

Economics Journals

Business Week (Weekly)
American Economic Review (Monthly)
Quarterly Journal of Economics

Political Science Journals

American Political Science Review (Quarterly)
Journal of Politics (Quarterly)
Political Affairs (Monthly)
Political Science Quarterly

These journals will be useful to you if you have a social science research project.

49————————————————

Once you have done your reading and made notecards from all the references you found, which of the following would you do next? Check one.

- Write a rough draft from your notecards. ☐
- Order your ideas or make an outline. ☐

Check your answer in **50**.

HOW MANY OF THESE RESEARCH WORKS DO YOU KNOW?

American Literature: A Journal of Literacy
   History, Criticism and Bibliography
Book Review Digest
Commentary
PMLA (Publications of the Modern Language
   Association)
New York Times Book Review
Poetry
English Journal
College English
Shakespeare Quarterly
Film Quarterly
Journal of Philosophy
The Music Index
The Musical Quarterly
Arts in Society
Arts Magazine
Index to Book Reviews in the Humanities
The Business Periodicals Index
The Business Index (on microform)

50————————————————

Order your ideas or make an outline. If you have good notecards, you can shuffle them around until you have an order of ideas that works as an outline. If you work better from a written outline, use your cards to make one.

⇨   Remember, this is an extremely important step. It requires trial and error, rearrangement, experimentation, and change. The better the outline you have, the less time you'll need to write your paper.

Go to 51.

51————————————————

The final stages of writing a rough draft, examining for errors, and then revising are all similar to the last steps of the **SLOWER** formula. One difference in writing a term paper is the use of footnotes and bibliographies. We don't have the space in this book to show you *how* to write a research paper. But we can guide you to three good books, any *one* of which will tell you what you need to know. They are:

Coyle, William, *Research Papers* (Fifth edition), Bobbs-Merrill, 1980.
Lester, James, *Writing Research Papers: A Complete Guide* (Fourth edition), Scott, Foresman and Company, 1984.
Turabian, Kathryn, *Student's Guide for Writing College Papers* (Third edition), University of Chicago Press, 1977.

Each of these three works provides a step-by-step method for writing the research paper and will do a much better job than we could here. They cover such areas as:

1. Choosing a topic
2. Forming a thesis
3. Making bibliographic cards
4. Using library resources
5. Note taking
6. Outlining
7. Writing the paper
8. Footnoting and Documenting
9. Bibliographies
10. Sample term papers in finished form

Check your library for these books; it will probably contain one or all of them. If not, your campus book store may carry one of them or someone there can order one of them for you.

You may not need any of these works mentioned. Generally, when a term paper is assigned, the instructor gives you the information you need or has the book store stock the term paper manual she wants you to use. But if all else fails, you know now where to look for help.

That's all for now.

CHAPTER SEVEN
Taking Examinations

GOALS AND OBJECTIVES

General Goals   When you complete this unit, you will

1. Believe that there is a general test-taking skill that can be learned
2. Have learned how to apply systematic procedures for more effective test taking
3. Be able to score higher on both objective and essay exams than you could previously, given the same knowledge
4. Have increased confidence when taking examinations

Specific Objectives   When you complete this unit, you will

1. Be able to schedule your time before beginning to work
2. Be able to organize your essay answers around a few important ideas
3. Be able to support your essay answers with examples and facts
4. Be able to search for and recognize the important word clues in examination questions and try to use them to guide your answers
5. Adopt a general strategy of answering the easier questions first and the more difficult later
6. Be more attentive to instructions and make an effort to read both instructions and questions carefully
7. Be able to use guessing as a technique of answering objective exam questions when it is profitable
8. Review your answers before considering the exam finished

You are not really just you. You are also a set of numbers locked away in a vault or punched on cards in a computer library. (Are you the holes or the bits of card?) Test scores and grades are a tag you wear; they are you in college, and they decide whether you will be ranked with the winners or with the losers.

I know, I know. You really *are* you. You are lovable and witty and sexy and incredibly good at ping pong or something. And grades are only part of the picture. Nevertheless, grades are competitive. If someone gets A's and B's, someone else will get D's and F's; if there are winners there will be losers. The purpose of this chapter is to teach you some of the skills needed to keep you in the winner's circle. Becoming more lovable, witty, and sexy is somthing you'll have to handle yourself.

Now, what do you want here?

1. A **quick course** in how to cram for exams ☐ Go to **1**.
2. A **super student's guide** to the art of taking exams ☐ Go to **2**.
3. Hints on how to score high on **true-false** and **multiple choice** tests ☐ Go to **8**.
4. Help with **essay** exams ☐ Go to **30**.
5. If you want (2), (3), *and* (4), go to **2**.

1———————————————

Cramming for an examination means that you do all or most of your studying for it in one big block of time, usually just before the exam. You literally cram all the information needed for the exam into your head in one last-minute orgy of intense studying. Most teachers and "how-to-study" books will tell you that cramming results in lower grades, wastes time, is useless and bad for your health, and leads to moral decay.

Nuts!

It is none of these things. Let's look at the good and bad side of it. On the negative side:

Negative side of cramming ⟩
1. **Fast in—fast out**. If you learn a large amount of memory material quickly you will probably forget it quickly. It takes time and much thoughtful play with ideas before they become a firm part of your memory.
2. **Battle fatigue**. If you have a series of examinations and you cram for all of them, the fatigue of the first few may destroy your ability to perform on the later ones. Cramming is much more fatiguing than steady, consistent, day-by-day study.
3. **The big picture**. Cramming may be helpful in keeping a few facts and words in your head long enough for you to pull them back out on the exam, but you may miss the big picture. Without steady, long-term, organized learning you may never see the important ideas and never obtain more than a surface feel for the subject studied. Even if you win, you lose.

4. **The tender self**. It is a good rule of life that you should never do anything that will make you think less of yourself. In the long run, you are all you have. Take care to build a strong, sure sense of who you are and what you are doing and why you are doing it. If cramming leaves you with the feeling that you have let yourself down, then it is bad for you.

For these reasons our advice is *DON'T CRAM*. But . . . if you must cram, here is a checklist to help you do it most effectively. Read it now. When you have an exam coming and you want to cram for it, start about one week before and check off each step as you do it.

The Week before the Exam—"Go" Week

1. Find out exactly what is required for the exam by doing the following:

   (a) Ask your instructor what the exam will cover and what kinds of questions will be used. _____

   (b) Ask your instructor what, if any, material will be omitted. _____

   (c) Make a list of what things you must know and rank them according to importance. _____

   (d) Get copies of previous exams. Your instructor will often be willing to help with this. _____

   (e) Talk to friends who have taken the course previously. Get their advice on what to study, what questions to expect, what the test will emphasize. (Very few instructors know their own biases.) _____

   (f) Get together a "study group" of some serious students and fire possible test questions at each other. Make certain the people you select are really interested in studying. _____

2. Organize yourself for maximum efficiency by doing the following:

   (a) Eat on schedule all week. _____

   (b) Get a normal amount of sleep every day all week. _____

   (c) Take time off from your out-of-school job or other activities. _____

   (d) Set aside your usual daily activities (TV, dates, hobbies) for *after* the exam. _____

   (e) Review the techniques given in this book to help you study and read more efficiently. _____

    (f) Review the techniques for taking various kinds of exams that are presented in this book. (If you want to do that now, turn to **2**.)   _____

    (g) Build up a positive mental attitude by reminding yourself of all the good consequences of succeeding on the exam and recalling past successes. Be positive. Think *up*.   _____

    (h) Plan an after-exam party, trip, or treat as a reward for your survival and success.   _____

3. Learn what you need to know for the exam.

    (a) Read the material. Don't take notes. Write in the book and underline.   _____

    (b) Review it. On each successive review skip those things you are most sure of.   _____

    (c) Recite. Buttonhole a friend or relative and tell him all about it. He'll think you're nuts, but do it anyway.   _____

    (d) Review the top priority items again at the last possible minute before entering the exam room.   _____

    (e) Don't let anyone bump your head.   _____

    (f) Never look back and have fun at the party.   _____

Again, the best advice is don't cram, but if this sort of thing is your style, go to it with a smile.

- If you are interested in the super student's guide to taking tests, go to **2**.
- If not, you are finished with this chapter. Good luck.

2————————————————

The super student **exam preparation** begins on the first day of class. Using the study principles outlined in other chapters of this book, he or she works steadily and methodically to understand the ideas presented in the course. In this way full advantage is taken of all the learning activities designed by the instructor. He finds the purpose in each part of the course, and through daily participation, he or she learns by doing rather than simply exposing himself to conversation. By exam time the course concepts are a meaningful and natural part of thinking. Most efforts are directed toward a search for the big picture. The little details fall quietly into place when they are needed.

It's a nice picture. But . . .

Regardless of the subject matter and the amount of studying a student has done, there are certain definite skills involved in taking examinations. Other sections of this book discuss study techniques; this one will concentrate on how to work most effectively during the actual exam.

Now, what is the first and most important step in test taking? Think about it.

Write your answer here, then turn to 3 to see if we agree.

3——————————————————————

The first and most important rule of test taking is "*be there*." About half of the entering freshmen in American colleges and universities never graduate. In most junior college courses fewer than half of the students who originally enrolled will still be there for the final exam.

The majority of those who fail college courses do so because they have not even taken the required examinations, not because they failed the exam.

We cannot give you a sure-fire formula for success, but we do know the easiest way to fail: quit. Perseverance, hanging on a little longer, trying just once more, will not get you an A grade by itself but it can keep you moving forward toward your goals.

The first step in test taking is to *be there;* be on time, be ready. Bring whatever you need for the test—pencils, paper, eraser. Bring notes, course outlines, books, dictionaries, or whatever aids are allowed. Come early and be prepared to stay as late as you are permitted.

Now, there you sit, test in hand. What next? Do you:

☐   (a) Get to work on the first question immediately?
☐   (b) Read the directions?
☐   (c) Read all test questions before you start?

Think about it, check an answer and go to 4 to continue.

4——————————————————————

The best answer is (b). **Read the directions.** Read them slowly and carefully. Pay attention to every detail. If the instructions are not clear or seem to have a double meaning, ask your instructor to explain them.

Here is an exercise in following directions. First, read over each of the 10 steps following.

1. Write your name here. _____

2. Add 2 and 3 and write the answer in the blank. _____

3. Add 6 to that answer and write the result here. _____

4. Multiply that answer by 2 and write the product in this blank. _____

5. Subtract 2 from the last answer and write it here. _____

6. Divide the last answer by 4 and write the result in the blank. _____

7. Add 10 and write it here. _____

8. Multiply by 3 and write it here. _____

9. Subtract 10 and write it here. _____

10. Subtract 1 from 2, place it in the first blank and do not complete any of the other nine items above.

Now, follow the directions given in step 10.
Finished? Check your answer in 5.

5 _____

If you followed directions, you will have written the number 1 in the first blank (where it calls for your name) and nothing in the others. The directions said to read over all 10 steps *first* and then follow the directions. Item 10 is the key instruction. Not following instructions will result in a great amount of wasted time.

The following kinds of information may be included in exam instructions:

1. **Time**. How much time is available for answering the questions? Is it a speed test requiring that you work as fast as possible, or can you work leisurely? Is the test divided into parts that have separate time limits? Time information is valuable in helping you decide how to spend *your* time most effectively.

2. **Choices**. What choices do you have in answering the exam questions? Must you answer all questions or may you skip some? Is there a choice of essay topics? Can you choose the order in which you answer questions or must you follow the sequence they are in?

Of course, you can always choose your answers to the questions, but on many tests, you may also decide which questions to answer.

3. **Form**. What form should your answer take? Should you check, circle, or underline a word, darken a space on an answer sheet, fill in words, letters, sentences, or phrases? How do you indicate true and false—T/F, +/0, A/B, yes/no, or write out the words? Are you going to write an essay or a paragraph? How long? Must the answer you choose be the exact answer, or can it be approximately correct? Must you include supporting facts? Must you show how you arrived at the answer? The instructor who grades the test will be expecting a certain kind of answer. Give precisely what he or she wants.

4. **Scoring**. Will some questions count more than others in the total exam score? If so, what is the relative importance of questions? Will the final exam grade be the sum of the correct answers, or will incorrect answers be counted against you? Are incorrect guesses penalized? Knowing how the test will be scored can also help you decide on the most effective use of your time.

5. **Aids**. May you use a scratch paper? Are calculators permitted? May you consult a dictionary, thesaurus, or other reference books? Are you permitted to use your textbook, class notes, outline, or other assistance? This kind of information should be obtained many days, even weeks, before the examination. If some important aid is allowed on the test and you come without it, you may be walking into a disaster.

To test your ability to recognize these kinds of information, read each of the following test instructions and indicate on the right the kind of information supplied.

Time
Choices
Form
Scoring
Aids

1. Papers will be graded for errors in mechanics as well as errors of fact. You may use your class notes.

    (a) _____
    (b) _____

2. Within the 2-hour time limit you are required to write two (2) essays. Write an essay on question 1 and choose one of the other questions for your second essay. Answer them in the order given.

    (a) _____
    (b) _____
    (c) _____

3. Write your name in the blank at the top of all pages. Put all objective answers in the space provided; essay answers are to be put in your bluebooks. Be certain your name is on every bluebook. Essays count 50 points each.

(a) _____
(b) _____

4. Answer eight of the following 12 questions. 40 points total, as indicated. You have 1 hour.

(a) _____
(b) _____
(c) _____

5. Essay questions (answer one).

(a) _____
(b) _____

6. Each of the questions below consists of one word followed by five words or phrases. You are to select the one word or phrase whose meaning is closest to that of the word in capital letters. Do not guess.

(a) _____
(b) _____

7. Each passage is followed by questions based on its content. After reading it, choose the best answer to each question and darken the corresponding space on the answer sheet. Answer all questions on the basis of what is stated or implied in the passage.

(a) _____
(b) _____

8. In this part of the test you will be asked questions about a map, a table, and a graph. Pick out the best answer to each question and mark the space for that answer. You will have 15 minutes. You are not expected to finish in the time allowed.

(a) _____
(b) _____
(c) _____

9. Answer true or false to each of the following questions. Indicate your answer with a T or F in the right margin.

(a) _____

10. Please write your answer, using capital letters, in the space provided to the left of the question. No notes or references may be used.

(a) _____
(b) _____

When you have completed each of these, compare your answers with the correct answers in **6**.

6————————————————

1. ". . .will be graded for errors. . ."
   (In other words don't guess.)   (a) Scoring
   ". . .may use class notes"   (b) Aids
2. ". . .2-hour time limit. . ."   (a) Time
   ". . .write two essays. . ."   (b) Form
   ". . .choose one of the other. . ."
   "Answer them in the order. . ."   (c) Choices
3. "write your name in. . ."
   "Put all answers in the space. . ."
   "essay answers are to be put in bluebooks"   (a) Form
   ". . .50 points each."   (b) Scoring
4. "Answer 8 of 12. . ."
   (Don't answer all 12.)   (a) Choices
   "40 points total"   (b) Scoring
   ". . .1 hour"   (c) Time
   (That's about 7 minutes each.)
5. "Essay questions"   (a) Form
   "Answer one"   (b) Choices
6. "Select the one word. . ."   (a) Form
   "Do not guess."
   (Usually means that points will be de-
   ducted for wrong answers)   (b) Scoring
7. ". . .darken the space. . ."
   ". . .on the basis of what is stated. . ."   (a) Form
   "Answer all questions. . ."
   (Omitted questions will count against   (b) Choices
   you.)
8. ". . .mark the space. . ."   (a) Form
   ". . .15 minutes."   (b) Time
   "You are not expected to finish. . ."
   (This means you really must hustle. Your
   score is the number correct.)   (c) Scoring
9. ". . .with a T or F in the right margin."
   (Use T and F. Do not write it out or use
   some other symbol. Answer in the right
   margin.)   (a) Form
10. ". . .using capital letters. . ."
    (Print not script.)
    ". . .in the space to the left. . ."   (a) Form
    "No notes or references. . ."   (b) Aids

We will discuss the most effective way of working on different kinds of exams in the next few sections of this chapter.

To continue, go to **8**.

7————————————————

Hi. I'm resting in here.

8————————————————

Taking Objective Tests

Almost any question can be labeled as objective or subjective. These words refer to what happens when the test is graded. An **objective exam** is one where the instructor's opinions and values are not a factor in grading. A **subjective** or **essay exam** is graded on the basis of his or her personal feelings and biases. The range of answers is wide open for both style and content. But with an objective exam, everyone with a grading key will agree on the correct answer to a question. Objective grading is a mechanical process and, in fact, is often done by machine. The simplest varieties of objective tests include true-false, multiple choice, completion or fill-in, matching, and problem questions.

Your job on an objective exam is to choose the best answer or alternative from those listed. You may be asked to select a single word or short phrase to complete a given sentence correctly. You may need to recall or recognize words, facts, or names. Unfortunately, not all test questions are well written and you may be forced to guess at what the instructor wants.

What is the most common reason students fail objective tests? Can you guess?

Write your answers here and then check it in **9**.

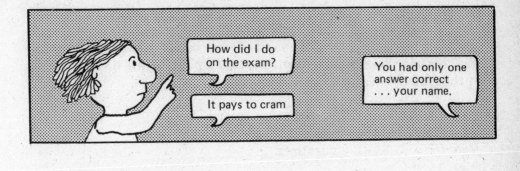

9————————————————

Most people would guess that failure results from lack of knowledge. Not always. Research studies show that your *ability to reason* with what you know is even more important than what you know. When taking tests, it is important that you be able to read and interpret questions correctly if you are to succeed.

To help you score as high as possible on all exams, we have devised a plan of attack called **SCORER**. Each letter in the word stands for an important rule in test taking. **SCORER** is based on the experience of many teachers and students and on research findings—we think it can work for you.

> S = **Schedule** your time
> C = **Clue** words
> O = **Omit** the difficult questions
> R = **Read** carefully
> E = **Estimate** your answers
> R = **Review** your work

Read SCORER again, slowly, then go to **13**.

10————————————————

The first letter in **SCORER** reminds you to **Schedule your time**.

Consider the exam as a whole. How long is it? How many sections? How many questions? Are there especially easy or very difficult sections or questions? Estimate roughly the time needed for each section. **Schedule** your time.

For example, in a 50-minute test containing 20 questions you can spend about

$$50 \div 20 \text{ or } 2\tfrac{1}{2} \text{ minutes}$$

on each question. If you start at 9 a.m. you should be one-third finished by 9:17, halfway by 9:25, working on question 40 by 9:40. If you lag much behind these times, you will run out of time before you finish the test.

Try this one. Your history exam starts at 1 p.m. Paging through it you find that it has three parts:

Part I   50 multiple-choice questions
Part II   30 true-false questions
Part III   3 essay questions

You are allowed 3 hours to do the test. What do you do now?

(a) Spend 1 hour on each part.   ☐ Go to **11**.
(b) Divide the number of questions into 3 hours and
     spend your time evenly on all.   ☐ Go to **12**.
(c) Punt.   ☐ Go to **14**.

11

Excellent. That is a good first guess. You now have a way to check your progress on the test. However, your scheme ignores the fact that some parts of the test may be much more difficult than others.

Suppose that Part I is worth 100 points, Part II is worth 75 points, and Part III is worth 50 points. Now how would you divide the 3 hours? You have 30 seconds to do it. GO!

Write out your answer here.

12

Not quite. This kind of scheduling of time assumes that every question is equally difficult. They probably are not. And I'll bet, knowing history teachers, that the three essay questions will count a lot more in the final score than true-false questions.

Go back to **10** and try another answer.

Then check in **15** for more.

MACHINE-SCORED TESTS

One advantage (for the instructor) of objective tests is that they can be corrected quickly and automatically by a computer or other device. Here are a few hints that may keep you from making serious errors.

1. Use the correct pencil. Most of these answering schemes require a special pencil. Bring it with you.
2. Completely fill the answer space and only that space.
3. If you must erase, do it completely. Be careful not to tear or fold the card or answer sheet.
4. Don't mark two answers. The questions will be counted incorrect automatically.
5. Be certain you mark your answer in the correct space. Mark answer number 16 for question 16.

13————————————————

Without peeking, write in what each letter stands for.

    S = _____
    C = _____
    O = _____
    R = _____
    E = _____
    R = _____

Check your answer by comparing with **9**. Then hop to **10** and we will look at each rule in detail.

14————————————————

Does that choice mean you feel a little lost? Relax. We'll find you.

Scheduling your time means that you find some scheme to pace yourself. Hopefully, the scheme will be based on the difficulty of different parts of the exam. No fancy math is needed; you make an educated guess on how to divide your time.

Return to **10** and try it.

15——————————————

If Part I is worth more than the average, play the odds, give it more time. Instead of

Part I—60 min		Part I—80 min		Part I—75 min
Part II—60 min	try	Part II—60 min	or	Part II—60 min
Part III—60 min		Part III—40 min		Part III—45 min

Now, suppose you are a super whiz on true-false questions but very slow on essay writing. What would be a better scheme?
Write your answer in this space.

Check your answer in **16**.

16——————————————

If you need less time on Part II (true-false questions) and more time on Part III (essay questions), then adjust again. Instead of

Part I—80 min		Part I—75 min
Part II—60 min	try	Part II—45 min
Part III—40 min		Part III—60 min

The important thing is to get a schedule that is reasonable for *you* and use it. A good schedule will help you make the best use of your time. It is a deadly mistake to trot leisurely through one part of an exam and be forced to sprint through the rest. When time is up you may find yourself an exhausted, mind-blown wreck spraying stupid mistakes in all directions. *Scoring high on tests starts with scheduling your test time.*
Now, go to **17** for rule 2 of **SCORER**.

17——————————————

The second letter in **SCORER** reminds you to watch for **clue words**.
Almost every question has built-in clues to what is wanted. In a true-false test the instructor must make up questions that are absolutely true or absolutely false. If she asks

"An unhappy childhood produces a neurotic adult. (True or false?)"

she has a question she cannot grade. The more you know about psychology the more difficult this question is to answer. It is sometimes true, sometimes not; true for some people, false for others. She is more likely to phrase it

"An unhappy childhood *always* produces a neurotic adult."

or

"An unhappy childhood *never* produces a neurotic adult."

or

"An unhappy childhood *sometimes* produces a neurotic adult."

The first two are clearly false and the last is clearly true. The words *always*, *never*, and *sometimes* are called clue words. They trim a big, sweeping general statement down to question size.

Try this: Modify the statement "Men are taller than women" so that it is clearly true or clearly false. Write your answer here:

Check it in **18**.

MATCHING QUESTIONS

In a matching question you must correctly link up two items of information. For example,

_____	(1) Winston S. Churchill	(a) Russian dictator
_____	(2) Robert F. Kennedy	(b) U.N. Ambassador
_____	(3) Joseph Stalin	(c) British Prime Minister
_____	(4) Adlai Stevenson	(d) Senator and Attorney General
		(e) Secretary of State

1. Read both columns quickly.
2. Start at the top of the left column and compare the first item in the right column.

3. When you get a match, put the appropriate letter in the space provided.
4. Do the *easy ones first*. Get all the matches you are sure of.
5. Cross out those entries in both columns.
6. Repeat the process with those that remain.
7. *Be neat*. This can get messy if you let it.

18————————————————

Try,

"*All* men are taller than *all* women."	False

or

"*Some* men are taller than women."	True

or

"Men are *never* taller than women."	False

or

"Men are *usually* taller than women."	True

or

"Men are *sometimes* taller than women."	True

The clue words are *all, some, never, usually, sometimes*. These words are a key to answering objective test questions.

Here is a list of clue words, arranged in families:

A215

Clue words			
All	Always	More	Best
Every	Invariably	Equal	Good
Many	Often	Less	Bad
Most	Usually		Worst
Some	Some-times		
Few	Seldom		
None	Never		

Read this list carefully.
In the following sentences underline the clue words.

1. People engaged in learning tasks always reach a plateau.
2. Learning invariably involves a change in the behavior of the learner.

3. All psychologists agree that learning is a response to stimuli.
4. Intelligence is probably just the ability to think clearly and to remember what has been learned.
5. Mental disorders are often caused by physical illness.

Check your answers in **19**.

19————————————————

You should have underlined <u>always</u>, <u>invariably</u>, <u>all</u>, <u>probably</u>, and <u>often</u>.

Some clue words such as *all, every, none, exactly, always,* and *never* indicate that the statement is absolutely true. Exceptions are not allowed. If they appear in a statement, it must be true in every case to be true at all. For example,

"All squares have four equal sides."
(That's part of a definition.)

"Every insect has six legs."
(If it has more or less than six, it is not an insect.)

"Politicians are invariably dishonest."
(That means there has never been an honest politician. We're not certain, but we think this is false.)

Other clue words such as *many, most, some, usually, few,* or *often* are qualifiers. They indicate a limited range of truth.

"Some apples are green."
(Sure, some are also yellow, pink, and even red.)

All clue words are red lights for test takers. When you see one, STOP and learn what it is telling you.

The second rule of **SCORER** means:

1. **Find the CLUE words**. Look for them in every question statement, they are usually present.
2. **Circle or underline them**.
3. See how they change the *meaning of the statement*.
4. Use them to help you to decide the truth or falsity of the statement.

Except for statements in science and mathematics, or in definitions, statements that do not contain qualifying clue words are generally false. But don't depend on it; most instructors are shifty and clever.

Turn back to **18** and read that list again. Then go to **20**.

20———————————————————————

The third letter in **SCORER** reminds you to **omit the difficult questions**.

A test is not some sort of semifatal illness you fall into; it is a battle to be planned, fought, and won. You size up the enemy, look at the terrain, check out his artillery, develop your strategy, and attack at the place you have the best chance of success. The **O** rule in **SCORER** says that to score high on tests you should find the easiest questions and answer them first. Omit or postpone the more difficult ones until later.

The procedure for an objective exam is the following:

1. Move rapidly through the test.
2. When you find an easy question or one you are certain of, answer it.
3. Omit the difficult ones on this first pass.
4. When you skip a question, make a mark in the margin (— or ✓). (Do not use a red pencil or pen. Your marks could get confused with the grader's marks.)
5. Keep moving. Never erase. Don't dawdle. Jot brief notes in the margin for later use if you need to.
6. When you have finished the easy ones, return to those with marks (— or ✓) and try again.
7. Mark again those answers you are still not sure of. Change the — to + or ✓ to ✓✓.
8. In your review (that's the last **R** in **SCORER**) you will go over all the questions time permits, first the ✓✓, then the ✓, then the unmarked.

Read these procedures again, then go to **21** for a short quiz on them.

21———————————————————————

The procedures for taking an **objective test** are:

(Complete these sentences.)

(1) Move _____ through the test.

(2) Answer the _____ questions first.

(3) _____ the more difficult questions.

(4) When you skip a _____ question, be sure to make a _____ in the margin.

(5) Keep _____. Never _____.

(6) After answering the _____ questions return

and _____ the _____ questions.

(7) _____ them again if you are still _____.

(8) When you review the test, go over the _____

questions first, then the _____, and finally the

_____ .

If you were unsure of any of these, return to **20** to check your answers; otherwise go to **22**.

22―――――――――――――――――

Here is a sample test with marked and double-marked questions and underlined clue words.

✓	<u>Every</u> nation with per capita income over $1000 has a capitalistic economy.	T	Ⓕ
	A nation can <u>never</u> consume more than it produces in <u>any</u> given year.	T	Ⓕ
✓✓	<u>Any</u> improvements in your house adds to the GNP in <u>any</u> given year.	Ⓣ	F
	A state constitutional convention may <u>only</u> be called by a majority vote of the people.	T	Ⓕ
✓	The basic effect of a tariff is <u>usually</u> to divert resources away from their <u>most</u> efficient uses.	Ⓣ	F

When you read a question on the first pass and decide to delay answering it until later, you are taking advantage of a marvelous property of the human brain. The difficult question is dropped into a quiet corner of the mind to soak or incubate. While you are working on the "easy" questions, a portion of your subconscious, with no effort from you, will be busily searching for a clue to the difficult question you omitted. Many different possible solutions will be dredged up, tried on for size, and discarded.

The human mind has the ability to perform many complex tasks simultaneously with no conscious effort. All that is required is that you drop the problem in, request an answer, give it plenty of soak time, relax, and expect it to happen. How well this process works will depend on how much information and how many concepts you have managed to store while studying; how free you can keep your mind from tensions, doubts, and other hang-ups; and how much soak time you allow. The more you practice *omitting the difficult questions,* the better you will get at it.

Now go to **23** and continue.

23

The fourth letter of **SCORER** reminds you to **read carefully.**

As we have already explained, it is very important that you read the directions carefully before you begin. It is also very important that you read each question completely and with care.

1. **Read all of the question**. Many students, because they are careless or rushed for time, read only part of the question and answer it on the basis of that part. For example, consider the statement

   Supreme Court decisions are very effective in influencing attitudes.

   If you disagree with some Supreme Court decisions, you may mark it false after reading the first six words. The political scientist knows it is true. He is not asking you whether the Court is doing a good job, only what the effects of its decisions are.
2. **Read the question as it is**. Be careful to interpret the question as the instructor intended. Don't let your bias or expectation lure you into a false reading. For example, the statement

   Once an American, always an American.

   may be marked true by a superpatriot who believes it should be true. Legally, it is not true.
3. **Read it logically**. If the statement has several parts, all parts must be true if the statement is to be true. The statement

   George Washington was elected President because he was a famous film star

   is false. (Not in 1776. Today it might be possible.) The statement

   Chlorine gas is a greenish, poisonous, foul-smelling, very rare gas used in water purification

   is false. (It is not rare.)

Go to **24** for a quick quiz on rule 4 in **SCORER**.

24——————————————————

Complete these sentences. Refer to **23** for help if you need it.

The fourth letter of **SCORER** reminds you to _____

_____

It is important that you (1) _____ _____ of the question, (2)

_____ the question as it is, and (3) read it _____ .

The statement

All bloops are zingy because most apples are purple

is _____ (true or false) because all parts of a statement must

be _____ if the statement is true.

Turn to **25** for the next **SCORER** rule.

MULTIPLE CHOICE QUESTIONS

Each multiple choice question is really a set of true-false questions.
For example, the question

Ben Franklin was born in

(a) 1706
(b) 1760
(c) 1806
(d) 1860

is equivalent to the set of statements

(a) Ben Franklin was born in 1706
(b) Ben Franklin was born in 1760
(c) Ben Franklin was born in 1806
(d) Ben Franklin was born in 1860

where only one of this set is true.

Treat the multiple choice question as a set of true-false statements. The only difference is that one may be more nearly true than

the others, rather than absolutely true. The best strategy is to eliminate all that are clearly false and only consider the rest.

> (1860?—a grown man in 1900?
> 1806?—Lincoln's age?   1760?—
> 16 years old in 1776?)

25

The **E** in **SCORER** reminds you to **Estimate**.

Your instructor may never admit it, but you can go a long way on an objective exam by **guessing**.

On most true-false or multiple choice tests your final score is simply the number you answer correctly. Wrong answers are ignored. There is no penalty for guessing. On some tests you may have points subtracted from your score for wrong answers. *Be certain you know how the test will be scored.* If the test directions do not make it perfectly clear, ask your instructor.

1. If there is no penalty for guessing, be certain you *answer every question* even if you must *guess*.
2. If you have plenty of time, proceed as we have already outlined: omit or postpone the difficult questions, answer the easy ones first, return to the difficult ones later. Guess at any you do not know. (But be careful. Your instructor may be upset if you start flipping a dime and shouting "Heads!" and "Tails!" during the exam.)
3. If the test is a long one and you are pressed for time, answer the easy ones, guess at the difficult ones and place a ✓ in the margin nearby. Return to the ✓ questions when you have finished and reexamine them. You may want to change your guess.
4. If guessing is penalized, then do not guess on true-false questions and make an educated guess on multiple-choice questions only if you can narrow the possibilities down to two. Guess at completion or fill-in questions if you have any idea of what the answer is. Part of a correct answer may earn you some credit.

"Guestimating" is an important part of test taking.

Here are two sets of test instructions. In the blank at the right, insert

(a) If you would GUESS
(b) If you would NOT GUESS

1. This is a timed test. You're not expected to finish. Your score will be the number correct. _____

2. Mark each answer True (T) or False (F). For every incorrect answer you will be penalized one point. _____

Number 1 should be answered (a) because you will *not* be penalized for mistakes. Number 2 should be answered (b) because you *would* be penalized for any mistakes.

Now go to **26**.

26————————————————

The last letter in **SCORER** is a reminder to **Review** your work.

Use every minute that is available to you. Anyone who leaves the exam room early is either very foolish or superconfident. **Review** everything you have done.

1. Return to the double-checked (✓✓) difficult questions. Reread them. Look for clue words. Look for new hints. Then go to the ✓ questions and finally to the unmarked ones if there is still time.
2. Don't be too eager to change answers. Change only if you have a good reason for changing.
3. Be certain you have considered all questions.
4. PRINT your name on the test. If there are separate sheets, print your name on each sheet.

It is most important to build up your knowledge and understanding of the subject through systematic study, reading, and class work. Other sections of this book will help you there. **SCORER** is designed to help you do your best with what you know.

Now, trilly on off to **27** for a quiz.

27————————————————

Write a brief statement telling what each letter in **SCORER** stands for. List the actions each step involves. Ready? OK, wind your mind, here we go.

S = _____
_____

C = _____
_____

O = _____
_____

R = _____
_____

E = _____
_____

R = _____

Compare your answer with that in **28**.

28──────────────────────

S = **Schedule** your time. Look over the entire test and make a rough estimate of the time you should spend on each part. *Pace yourself.* See **10**.

C = **Clue words**. Find the clue words, such as *some, every, usually, always,* and *never,* that are used to make the question statement clearly true or false. See **17**.

O = **Omit** the difficult questions. Omit or postpone the difficult questions on the first pass through the test. *Do the easy ones first* and mark the others with a ✓ in the margin so that you may return to them later. See **20**.

R = **Read** carefully. *Read the directions. Read the questions* completely and with care. Look for the instructor's intention and answer the question accordingly. See **23**.

E = **Estimate**. If there is no penalty for incorrect answers, then be certain you *answer all questions. Guess* at those you do not know. See **25**.

R = **Review**. *Reread and reexamine* the most difficult questions, and then the easier ones. *Review* all questions if time permits. See **26**.

If you had trouble with any of these return to the frame indicated and review. Otherwise, check the statement below that best describes what you want to do next.

1. Give me some practice exercises on objective exams.

☐ Go to **P1** on page 249.

2. I need help with essay exams.

☐ Go to **30**.

3. I need a rest.

☐ Close the book and relax. Come back here when you're rested.

4. Tell me a joke.

☐ Try **29**.

29————————————————

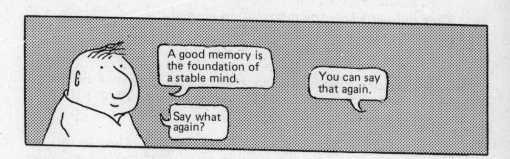

On to **30**.

30————————————————

Taking Essay Tests

An **essay examination** is a subjective exam in which the student responds to a question by writing a complete and original statement. The answer may range from a single sentence to an essay of many pages. Most such exams involve the writing of a short essay of a few paragraphs. It usually requires a demonstration of the student's understanding of the ideas he has learned, rather than a simple statement of fact or a feat of memory.

Why do people fail essay exams? Can you guess? Try. Write your answer here:

Go to **31** to check your answer.

CENTER FOR TEACHING AND LEARNING
P. O. Box H
Stanford, California 94305

31————————————————

You probably guessed that people fail exams because they do not know the material or have not studied. If so, you are wrong. In a recent research study, instructors were asked to list the most common reasons students in their classes failed essay exams. The five reasons listed most often were (in order of importance):

1. The students could not reason correctly.
2. Their writing was not clear and understandable. (Not handwriting, but the way they expressed their ideas.)
3. Answers were not organized logically.
4. They misinterpreted the questions.
5. They did not know the information needed.

As one history instructor expressed it,

> The ones that fail are just not equipped to do the job. They try—they read the assignments, they listen, they understand—but they cannot put it all together on an exam.

To help you "put it all together" and score high on essay exams, we have devised a plan of attack called **SCORER**. **SCORER** was discussed earlier in the section of this unit with objective tests. In this section we will show how **SCORER** can be applied to essay exams. Each letter in the word **SCORER** stands for an important rule in test taking. **SCORER** is based on the experience of many teachers and students and on research findings. These things all happen continuously during test taking.

S = **Schedule** your time and your work
C = **Clue** words
O = **Omit** the difficult questions
R = **Read** carefully
E = **Estimate** your answers
R = **Review** your work

Read **SCORER** again, then go to **34**.

32————————————————

The first letter in **SCORER** reminds you to **schedule** your time and *schedule* your work.

Scheduling your time means that you pace yourself through the test. There is nothing more agonizing than to find yourself with 10 minutes to go and 30 minutes of work to do. To prevent this sort of disaster,

1. Read all of the exam before you start.
2. Determine how much each question is worth in the final score.
3. Work out a rough time schedule.

For example, suppose your 2-hour English Literature final has six essay questions, one worth 50 points and the remaining five worth 10 points each. How do you divvy up the 2 hours?

Work it out roughly. It should not take more than 30 seconds to get an estimate.

Look in **33** for our answer.

33————————————————

The big one is worth 50 points and the rest are worth 50 points. Spend an hour on the big one and an hour on the rest, or 12 minutes on each of the five shorter questions.

Now suppose that the big one is on a topic you know very well and two of the shorter ones are on topics you know little about. How would you pace yourself?

Check your answer in **35**.

34————————————————

Without peeking, write in what each letter in **SCORER** stands for.

S = _____

C = _____

O = _____

R = _____

E = _____

R = _____

Check your answer by comparing with **31**. Then go to **32** and we will look at each rule in detail.

35————————————————

A reasonable procedure would be to spend 50 minutes on the big question, 12 minutes on the three easy short ones, and 17 minutes each on the two difficult short ones. Take 10 minutes from the easy one and spend it on the more difficult.

There is no need for a lot of math here—make rough estimates. If the question asks for a simple list, a few facts, or a short answer, give it less time. If it calls for a discussion or long answer, give it more time.

In essay exams you also schedule your work. Essay exams are wide open for your imagination and creativity. For maximum effectiveness it is absolutely vital that you **plan your answer**. Organize before you write; it will save time and get you a higher score.

Go to **36** for some hints.

36————————————————

How to schedule your work.

1. Get an **outline** started. List the important points to cover—facts, names, dates, research. Write them down. This is the *core* of your answer.
2. **Order** the points. Number them into a sequence (a map of what you will say, a direction for your answer to go). Find some sort of order—logical, chronological, or whatever works best.
3. **Add support** to the *core*. Note any **examples** or *facts* that support these main statements. Each main statement with its support will be a separate paragraph in the final essay.
4. **Be direct** when you write. Get directly to the *core*. Don't start off with a long, slow, rambling build-up or a philosophical discussion. *Move it.*
5. **Use signals** to let your instructor know what you are going to say.

   There are three reasons why . . .
   First, . . . Second, . . . Third, . . .
   In early Greece. . . . But in Rome . . .
   Finally, ...

Remember, your instructor may be reading a hundred of these exams and hating every minute of it. Help him out. Be organized, be direct, get right to the *core*. He will see immediately what you are doing and he will appreciate it—even if your answer is wrong!

There is something unsatisfactory about the following answer. Do you see what it is?

Question: Discuss the role of Thomas Jefferson in the development of American higher education.

Answer: *"The Role of Thomas Jefferson in the Development of American Higher Education*

In colonial times higher education was a privilege of the few. It was designed to prepare young men for the ministry. Among the many people who played an important role in its development was Thomas Jefferson. . . ."

Try rewording it. Then check your answer in **37**.

NEGATIVES

Avoid **double negatives**. When you must interpret one, for example,

He was not without courage in the face of battle.
[Was he a coward or not?]

tackle it this way:

1. Eliminate the two negatives:

   "He was with courage in. . . ."

2. Rephrase it:

   "He was courageous in. . . ."

3. Answer the question:

   "He was *not* a coward. . . ."

- Avoid double negatives in your own writing.
- Always put statements in positive form.
- Avoid

   "He did not think that history was very interesting."

Say

   "He thought history was dull."

Positive writing is easier to read and more forceful.

37————————————————————

A much better approach is to

1. Not rewrite the question
2. Get directly to the point

Try this:

> Answer: "Jefferson influenced American higher education in four
> important ways: first . . . As an example, ..."

No beating around the bush here. Notice the use of signal words to
telegraph the writer's intentions. Also note the use of examples to support the *core* ideas.

Complete these sentences describing the process of scheduling or
organizing your work on essay examinations.

Refer to **36** for help if you need it.

1. Get an _____ . List the _____ .

2. _____ these points.

3. Add _____ in the form of _____

   or _____ . Each main point will be a

   separate _____ .

4. Be _____ . Get directly to the _____ .

5. Use _____ to show your intent.

Check your answers in **38**.

38————————————————————

The process of scheduling or organizing your work on essay exams is:

1. Get an **outline**. List the *important points* or *ideas*.
2. **Order** these points.
3. **Add support** in the form of *examples* or *facts*. Each main point will
   be a separate *paragraph*.
4. **Be direct**. Get directly to the *core*.
5. **Use signals** to show your intent.

Go to **39** for the second rule of **SCORER**.

EXAM PANIC

What can you do if you panic during an exam?

You walk into the exam room and sit down, and you can already feel the tension rising. The old feelings return: tight chest, pounding heart, a sinking empty space in your stomach. Your palms sweat. You can't breath. Within a minute the test has been blocked out completely.

All of us experience exam panic to some extent, and the secret of working through it is **relaxation**. Try this:

1. Sit upright, breathe deeply and easily with your eyes closed. Rotate your shoulders to relax them. Drop your hands limply in your lap. **Focus on your breathing**. With each inhalation, draw peace and relaxation in like a drink of air. With each exhalation, feel tension pour out of your chest, abdomen, shoulders, wrists, and hands. Gradually assume control.

2. When you feel in control of this relaxation process, return to the test and read through each question carefully. If the answer comes quickly, fine. Write it down. If no immediate response comes, that is equally fine. Go on to the next question.

3. When you have completed this first pass through the exam, or sooner if you need it, close your eyes and again work on controlled breathing and tension release. Breathe out the tension built up by this first pass through the exam. When you are more relaxed, begin again with the unanswered questions. Read each one carefully. Answer if you can. Don't force an answer, you'll be coming this way again.

4. Repeat the process until either all of the questions have been answered or the exam time is up.

Every person experiences this kind of panic to some degree in some situations. Success depends not on fighting it, but on accepting your feelings, and learning to assume relaxed control.

39————————————————

The **C** in **SCORER** reminds you to find the **clue words**.

Every essay question contains certain words called **clue words** that tell you exactly what to do. Clue words are extremely important in essay questions. Your instructor will not usually ask you to "write a short essay on Socrates." Instead he might ask you to "contrast the philosophy of Socrates with that of the Ionians." *Contrast* is the clue word here. He has chosen this word because he wants a certain kind of answer. If he asks you to "list the parts of . . . ." he wants a *list,* not a story or an argument. *List* is the clue word here.

Circle the **clue words** in the following:

1. Review the factors that produce individual differences in man.
2. Compare Skinner's explanation of human behavior with that of Maslow.
3. Define secondary motivation.
4. Choose one research study on perception, describe it, and list its conclusions.
5. IQ and achievement are not directly related. Explain why this is so.

Check your answers in **40.**

40————————————————

The clue words are:

1. **Review**. The answer should be a summary of the important factors with comment and criticism.
2. **Compare.** You are being asked to show both the similarities and the differences between two explanations.
3. **Define.** You are being asked to give the formal meaning of a term, particularly to distinguish it from other similar terms that are closely related, such as primary motivation in this case.
4. **Choose** . . . **describe** . . . **list.** First, you are given a choice of topic. Second, *describe* requires that you give a detailed verbal picture of something in logical sequence or story form. Third, *list* means to finish with a numbered list of brief sentences.
5. **Explain.** The answer will be a logical accounting for some fact. You must state the cause of the fact and fit it into what you know.

Clue words are the key to high exam scores.
An essay game is a mental game in which the instructor subtly tells

you what he wants. Precision in word meanings is old hat to him, therefore you must be alert and learn precisely what they mean. Find the clue words, know exactly what they mean, then do exactly what is called for.

41 contains a list of the most common essay exam clue words and their meanings. Go there and read the list carefully.

41

Clue Word	Action Required
Analyze	Means to find the *main ideas* and show *how they are related* and why they are important.
Comment on	Means to *discuss, criticize,* or *explain* its meaning as completely as possible.
Compare	Means to show both the *similarities* and *differences*.
Contrast	Means to compare by showing the *differences*.
Criticize	Means to give your *judgment* or reasoned *opinion* of something, showing its *good and bad* points. It is not necessary to attack it.
Define	Means to give the *formal meaning* by distinguishing it from related terms. This is often a matter of giving a memorized definition.
Describe	Means to write a *detailed account* or verbal picture in a *logical sequence* or story form.
Diagram	Means to make a *graph, chart,* or *drawing*. Be sure you *label it* and add a *brief* explanation if it is needed.
Discuss	Means to describe giving the *details* and explaining the *pros and cons* of it.
Enumerate	Means to *list. Name* and *list* the main ideas one by one. Number them.
Evaluate	Means to give your *opinion* or some *expert's* opinion of the *truth or importance* of the concept. Tell the *advantages* and *disadvantages*.
Illustrate	Means to explain or make it clear by *concrete examples, comparisons,* or *analogies*.

Clue Word	Action Required
Interpret	Means to give the *meaning* using *examples* and *personal comments* to make it clear.
Justify	Means to give a statement of *why you think it is so.* Give *reasons* for your statement or conclusion.
List	Means to produce a *numbered list* of words, sentences, or comments. Same as *enumerate.*
Outline	Means to give a general summary. It should contain a *series of main ideas* supported by secondary ideas. *Omit minor details.* Show the *organization* of the ideas.
Prove	Means to show by *argument* or *logic* that it is true. The word "prove" has a very special meaning in mathematics and physics.
Relate	Means to show the *connections* between things, telling how one *causes* or is *like* another.
Review	Means to give a *survey* or *summary* in which you look at the *important parts* and *criticize* where needed.
State	Means to describe the *main points* in *precise* terms. Be *formal.* Use *brief, clear sentences.* *Omit details* or examples.
Summarize	Means to give a *brief,* condensed account of the *main ideas. Omit details* and examples.
Trace	Means to follow the *progress* or *history* of the subject.

This list is too long for most students to memorize, but try to remember the seven most often used clue words:

Most used clue words > **discuss, contrast, compare, criticize, define, describe, list**

Reread the above list with special attention to these seven words. Then go to **43**.

42

The third letter in **SCORER** reminds you to **omit the difficult questions**.

Read all of the examination before you begin writing. Note the easy questions, those you know the most about, are sure of, or are most interested in. Jot down facts, names, dates, comments on scratch paper or in the margin as you read along. Place a √ or other mark in the margin near these. Mark those that seem most difficult or time consuming with a √√ or other symbol.

Answer the easy ones first. Starting with an easy question gets you moving quickly and with confidence. A bit of early success will stimulate you to do a better job on later questions. On most exams even a few questions answered well can mean a passing grade.

While you write, your subconscious mind will be busy working on the other questions. From time to time a word or idea needed for some other question will pop into your head. Jot it down in the margin of the exam paper near that question. Expect that your mind will work on several things on different levels of awareness at the same time, and it will.

Omit or postpone the difficult questions on the first reading and answer the *easy questions first*.

Go to **44**.

MATH AND SCIENCE EXAMS

Most exams in mathematics and physical science involve problems where you must apply the concepts, knowledge, understanding, and techniques learned in the course to new situations. Here are some hints for problem exams.

1. Do the **easy ones first**.
2. **Read the problem**. Determine exactly what you are required to find. What does the answer look like? Is it a speed? A temperature? Or energy?
3. **Estimate the answer** before you begin to work the problem. It helps to have a rough idea of the size of the answer.
4. **Include the units** with all answers and *round* them to the proper place.
5. Your instructor will have worked problems in class and you may recall worked examples in your text. Try to see the exam problem as another example of a problem you have already solved or studied.
6. In preparing for problem exams, it is important that you **work many problems**. For most students the course grade or exam grade is directly proportional to the number of problems they do. Don't spend all of your study time on a few very difficult problems. Rather, do many of the easier ones until you are certain of your ability.

7. If the exam will require you to perform mathematical proofs or derivations, be certain you know which proofs may be required. **Drill** yourself on these before the test. Repeat each proof step by step until you remember each step and can quickly outline the proof.
8. See your instructor for **pre-exam help** when you need it, but come prepared with a list of specific questions. Show her your attempts at the problem, and she will be more willing to help.
9. **Go over every test afterward**. Learn how to do the problems you have missed. Science and math courses build an inverted pyramid of ideas. Anything you do not understand now will return to haunt you later in the course.

43

List the seven most used essay clue words and the actions they require.

Clue Word　　　　**Action Required**

＿＿＿＿＿＿＿＿　Means to ＿＿＿＿＿＿＿＿＿＿＿＿＿

＿＿＿＿＿＿＿＿＿＿＿＿＿＿＿＿＿＿

＿＿＿＿＿＿＿＿　Means to ＿＿＿＿＿＿＿＿＿＿＿＿＿

＿＿＿＿＿＿＿＿＿＿＿＿＿＿＿＿＿＿

＿＿＿＿＿＿＿＿　Means to ＿＿＿＿＿＿＿＿＿＿＿＿＿

＿＿＿＿＿＿＿＿＿＿＿＿＿＿＿＿＿＿

＿＿＿＿＿＿＿＿　Means to ＿＿＿＿＿＿＿＿＿＿＿＿＿

＿＿＿＿＿＿＿＿＿＿＿＿＿＿＿＿＿＿

＿＿＿＿＿＿＿＿　Means to ＿＿＿＿＿＿＿＿＿＿＿＿＿

＿＿＿＿＿＿＿＿＿＿＿＿＿＿＿＿＿＿

＿＿＿＿＿＿＿＿　Means to ＿＿＿＿＿＿＿＿＿＿＿＿＿

＿＿＿＿＿＿＿＿＿＿＿＿＿＿＿＿＿＿

＿＿＿＿＿＿＿＿　Means to ＿＿＿＿＿＿＿＿＿＿＿＿＿

＿＿＿＿＿＿＿＿＿＿＿＿＿＿＿＿＿＿

Write it out. Check your answer in **41**, then go on to **42**.

44————————————————————

The fourth letter in **SCORER** reminds you to **read carefully**.

Many students are in such a frantic hurry to start writing that they fail to read the exam. *Read carefully*.

Reading exams 1. Be certain to **read the instructions**. Find out if you have any options. Can any questions be omitted? How many? Which ones? How will the test be scored? Don't panic if those around you are already writing while you still read and organize. A few minutes spent here will save you time and increase your exam score later.

2. Read with an eye to the **teacher's preferences.** *Tell him what he wants to hear*. Does he like *quantity? Brief answers? Outlines? Lists?* Learn from earlier exams or from friends who have taken the course before what his biases and prejudices are—no need to be cynical. The point is that an exam is not the time to argue with him. Accept his point of view for the sake of the exam. If you strongly disagree with him about something, stop by next term and talk about it. You may both enjoy the visit.

3. **Read the question carefully**. *Answer what he asks*. Many students read the question quickly, spot a familiar word or name and start writing, pouring out words like a broken water pipe. They might spot the name *Roosevelt* and proceed to write an essay on F.D.R., piling in facts and opinions as they come to mind. But the question may have asked for a description of the U.S. economy in the years before he became President, a comparison of him with another President, or a list of his major achievements. The *clue words* are the key to what you should write.

Now, go to **45**.

45————————————————————

The fifth letter of **SCORER** reminds you to **estimate** your answers.

Guessing is a must on objective (true-false or multiple choice) exams, but it is very risky on essay exams. Here are a few hints.

1. **Don't guess on long essay exams**. If you are not prepared, the reader will know it no matter what you write. The best plan is to prepare before the exam—read, study, review, recite.

2. **Make educated guesses** on fill-in or very short answer questions unless wrong answers are penalized. It is usually true that two half-wrong answers are worth more points than one correct one. At least they may be worth *something*.

3. If you are not sure precisely what is needed, don't make a wild guess; instead try to **relate the question to the important core ideas** of the course. That is precisely what the instructor wants you to do. Always try to do it.

4. **Don't digress**. Don't be long-winded. *Don't pad your answer*. This is a waste of his time and yours. He will resent it and may become a bit prejudiced against your other answers or read the rest of your paper faster and miss your best work. He knows exactly what you are doing—he has done it himself!

Use examples to fill space if you are stuck with a shortage of "smarts."

Don't write notes to your instructor on the exam. If you have something to say, make an appointment to see him in his office.

Go to **46** for a little quiz.

46

As a review of the estimate rule of **SCORER** complete the following statements.
Turn to **45** for help if you need it.

1. Don't guess on _____ exams.

2. Make _____ _____ on short answer questions.

3. Relate the question to the _____ _____ _____
   _____ of the course.

4. Don't _____ your answer.

Check your answers in **45**, and then continue in **47**.

47

The last letter in **SCORER** reminds you to **review**.

It is vitally important on essay exams that you go back over your answer when you finish writing. It is so important that you should allot a few minutes to this review even if you haven't enough time to do all the writing you want. Reviewing could get you a better score than spending 3 to 5 more minutes on a difficult question. (You saved those till last, remember?)

Here is a checklist of questions to answer when you review.

1. Did you use *complete grammatical sentences?*
2. Did you follow the principles outlined in the section of this book on *Writing Short Papers?*
3. Did you *use examples?*
4. Is your name PRINTED on all separate parts of the exam?
5. Did you check spelling and punctuation?
6. Were you as direct as possible? Did you pad or digress?
7. Did you try to use originality?

Go to **48** for a review of **SCORER**.

48————————————————————

Write a list of brief statements telling what each letter in **SCORER** means for essay exams. Explain what action each rule involves.

S = _____
_____

C = _____
_____

O = _____
_____

R = _____
_____

E = _____
_____

R = _____
_____

Write it out, referring back to the text if you must.
Then turn to **49** to check your answer.

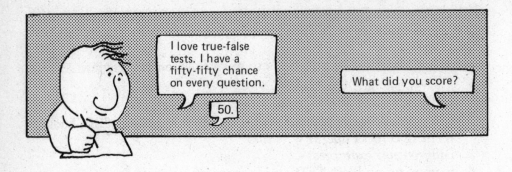

49

   S = **Schedule** your time and your work. *Outline* important parts. Get the *core*. Add *supporting* examples and facts.

       Be *direct*. Use *signals*. See **32**.

   C = **Clue words**. Look for clue words, such as contrast, compare, criticize, define, describe, discuss, and list.

       See **39**.

   O = **Omit** or postpone the difficult questions. Do the *easy questions first*. See **42**.

   R = **Read carefully**. Read instructions. Find out what the instructor wants. Read the questions. See **44**.

   E = **Estimate** your answers. Don't guess on long essay questions. Make educated guesses on short answer questions. Don't pad. Relate the question to a *core* of important ideas. See **45**.

   R = **Review** your work. Check *spelling, grammar,* and your *name.* Did you use *examples?* Were you *direct?*

       See **47**.

If you missed any of these, return to the frames indicated and review. Otherwise go to **50**.

50

Finally, a word about cheating.
   Don't.
   Whatever the pressure of opportunity, need for a good grade, or knowledge that others are doing it, don't be dishonest. Not because you might get caught and forced to leave school or be hurt in job references later, or because it is unfair to other students, or even because it is against the

rules or "bad." Stand away from it because it will build in you a negative view of yourself. You will think less of you and that is the greatest of losses.

Now, if you are a superstudent, you will want to go on to the practice exercises in **P1**. If you have already done the practice exercises for objective exams, go to **P9** on page 254.

Otherwise, you are finished with this chapter.

WORDS THAT END IN -ery/-ary AND -ify/efy

- There are only six common words in English that end in -ery. Here they are:

  cemetery   millinery   monastery
  distillery   confectionery   stationery

  Memorize these -ery words.
  All others pronounced this way end in -ary.

- There are only four common English words that end in -efy. Here they are:

  stupefy   putrefy
  liquefy   rarefy

  All others pronounced this way end in -ify.

Chapter 7 Practice Exercises

Practice exercises for objective (true-false or multiple-choice) exams begin in **P1**. Exercises for essay exams begin in **P9**.

P1 ——————————————

As a first review exercise go back over this chapter and circle all *clue* words.

When you finish, go on to **P2** for more practice.

P2 ——————————————

Complete the following quiz using the test-taking techniques described in this book.

Read each statement carefully and decide whether it is true or false. If it is true, place a T in the space at the left. If it is false, leave the answer space blank. Work fast. You have 1 minute.
Begin!

_____ (1) The **S** in **SQ3R** means "study."   (1) _____

_____ (2) When you read you must always think about   (2) _____
           what your eyes are doing.

_____ (3) Reading is probably the best way to build   (3) _____
           your vocabulary.

_____ (4) The **O** in **SCORER** means "organize."   (4) _____

_____ (5) Recitation is usually a valuable way to study.   (5) _____

_____ (6) Cramming leads inevitably to failure.   (6) _____

_____ (7) A true-false question including the word   (7) _____
           always is always false.

_____ (8) Guessing is often valuable on objective tests.   (8) _____

_____ (9) If part of a true-false question is false, it is all   (9) _____
           false.

_____ (10) A one-word answer is never a good idea.   (10) _____

Check your answers in **P4**.

P3————————————————

It is important that on any exam you stay alert and think clearly. The following quiz is designed to test your ability to think fast and logically and to follow instructions.

Answer each question by marking T for true or F for false in the answer space to the right.
Follow directions.
Work fast, you have 1 minute.
Go!

1. Answer this wrong: The earth is a cube.   _____

2. Answer this correctly: There are 50 stars and 14
                            stripes in the U.S. flag.   _____

3. Answer this wrong: Neither Brazil nor Italy is
                            a South American country.   _____

4. Answer this correctly: Both Brazil and Italy are
                              South American countries. _____

5. Answer this wrong: The statements "All lady-
                              bugs are female" and "some
                              barking dogs bite" are
                              false.   _____

When your head unwinds, go to **P5** and check your answers.

P4———————————————————————

Your quiz should look something like this:

____	(1)	The **S** in **SQ3R** means "study."	(1) ____
____	(2)	When you read you must *always* think about what your eyes are doing.	(2) ____
_T_	(3)	Reading is *probably* the best way to build your vocabulary.	(3) ____
____	(4)	The **O** in **SCORER** means "organize."	(4) ____
_T_	(5)	Recitation is *usually* a valuable way to study.	(5) ____
____	(6)	Cramming leads *inevitably* to failure.	(6) ____
____	(7)	A true-false question including the word "always" is *always* false.	(7) ____
_T_	(8)	Guessing is *often* valuable on objective tests.	(8) ____
_T_	(9)	If part of a true-false question is false, it is all false.	(9) ____
____	(10)	A one-word answer is *never* a good idea.	(10) ____

- Did you put your T marks on the left as required?
- Did you leave the answer space blank when the statement was false?
- Did you identify the *clue* words?
- Did you save the more difficult until last?
- Did you review?
- Did you schedule your time?
- Did you answer all questions, even if you had to guess?

Now turn to **P3** for another practice quiz.

P5———————————————

The proper answers are: (1) T, (2) F, (3) T, (4) F, (5) F.

Here is a list of common complaints often heard from students after objective exams. What rule in **SCORER** have they ignored in each case? (They may bring tears of recognition to your eyes. Don't blubber on the book.)

1. "I forgot to put my name on the test." ——————————————

2. "I ran out of time." ——————————————————

3. "I got hung up on a tough problem." ——————————————

4. "You mean we didn't need to do *all* of them?" ——————————

5. "I work too slow." ————————————————————

6. "I didn't notice that." —————————————————————

7. "The last part was easy? I never got to it." ————————————

8. "Well it was partly true, wasn't it?" ——————————————

9. "None of the answers were correct." ——————————————

10. "That wasn't fair. It was a trick question." ————————————

Check in **P7** for the correct answers.

P6———————————————

Read each of the following test instructions. In the blank at the right, insert (a) if you would GUESS, (b) if you would NOT GUESS, or (c) if you would GUESS if you can reduce the possibilities.

1. In this true-false test your score will be the number   ——
   correct.

2. This is a multiple-choice exam. Answer all questions. Your   ——
   final score will be the number correct minus the number
   wrong.

3. This is a 200-question true-false exam. You have 5 min-   ——
   utes. Mark questions T or F in the answer space given.
   You are not expected to finish.

4. For questions in this multiple-choice section choose the   ——
   answer that is most nearly correct. Your final score will be
   the number you answer correctly.

5. Fill in the word or phrase that best completes the statement. ____

6. Answer questions in the space provided. Do not guess. ____

7. In this 5-choice multiple-choice exam your final score will be the number correct minus one-fifth the number wrong. ____

Check your answers in **P8**.

P7———————————————

1. **Review**.
2. **Schedule** your time. (You didn't "run out of time." Everyone had the same amount of time. You neglected to use your time as effectively as you could.)
3. **Omit** the difficult.
4. **Read** carefully. (Why did he write the instructions if not to tell you something important?)
5. **Schedule** your time.
6. **Read** carefully.
7. **Schedule** your time.
   Omit the difficult. (You should have searched for the easy ones first.)
8. **Clue words.** (Partly true is all false.)
9. **Read** carefully.
   Clue words. (On a multiple-choice exam one of the statements will be more nearly true than the rest.)
   Estimate—Guess.
10. **Clue words.** (He is not tricking you; he is using the words precisely.)

Now go to **P8**.

P8———————————————

The answers to **P6** are: 1. (a), 2. (b), 3. (a), 4. (a), 5. (c), 6. (b), 7. (c). Refer to **25** if you had trouble with these.

In each of the following objective test statements identify the clue words by circling them.

1. Conflict between age and youth is inevitable in our modern culture.
2. Mental disorder is more likely to appear in adolescence than in childhood or old age.
3. In the United States no one wants to live with old people.

4. Psychologists are interested only in developing theories of human behavior.
5. Every human being follows the same stages of intellectual development.
6. All barking dogs bite.
7. Neurotic behavior is often learned in childhood.
8. Marijuana never leads to drug addiction.
9. Aggressive people are usually frustrated.
10. Inability to perceive reality may be a schizophrenic reaction.

Check your answers in **P10**.

P9————————————

Suppose you were given a 2-hour examination that had three parts worth 50 points, 30 points, and 20 points, respectively. How would you schedule your time?

Work out a rough estimate and then check your answer in **P11**.

P10————————————

The clue words in the statements in **P8** are

inevitable, more likely, no one, only, every, all, often never, usually, may

If you arrived here from frame **28**, go back to **30** on page 233.
If you want to review the procedures for taking essay exams, go to **P9**.
Otherwise, you are finished with this chapter.

P11————————————————

You have 120   minutes for 90 points
         or 12   minutes for 9 points
         or 4   minutes for 3 points

   A 10-point question should therefore be given about 12 or 13 minutes, a 30-point question should be given about 40 minutes, and a 50-point question should be given about 65 minutes. Allow a few minutes for reading instructions.
   Now suppose the 30-point section just happens to be on a topic you know very well and the other two are unfamiliar. How will you adjust your time schedule? No fancy math—"guesstimate."
   Check your guess with **P12**.

P12————————————————

Try adjusting from

Part I	50 points	65 minutes
Part II	30 points	40 minutes
Part III	10 points	13 minutes

   to

Part I	50 points	72 minutes
Part II	30 points	30 minutes
Part III	10 points	16 minutes

or even

Part I	50 points	75 minutes
Part II	30 points	25 minutes
Part III	10 points	20 minutes

   Don't spend a lot of time calculating how many minutes you have left. But *do* jot down the times when you should be finished with each part— that will serve as a general guide.
   Continue in **P13**.

P13————————————————

Underline the clue words in each of the following essay questions and describe the form of the answer that should be given.

1. List six causes of the Spanish-American War.

2. Summarize the role played by lobby groups in Washington.

3. Contrast Freud's view of the nature of man with Locke's.

4. Compare the philosophy and goals of fascism and communism.

5. Trace the development of the concept of monotheism in Western thought.

6. Debate the question "Is abortion morally defensible?" Discuss the use of abortion as a means of population control. Evaluate war and automobile use as population control devices.

7. Justify the use of the atom bomb in World War II.

8. A great scientist once wrote "With science one can explain everything except oneself." Interpret this sentence.

Turn to P15 for the correct answers.

P14————————————————

When you review your work after answering the questions on an essay exam, what things do you look for?
   List them at the top of the next page.

1. _____

2. _____

3. _____

4. _____

5. _____

6. _____

7. _____

Check your answers in **47**, then go to **P16** for another practice exercise.

P15————————————————————

1. **List**	The answer will be a numerical list in concise form.
2. **Summarize**	The answer will list the main points. It will be brief and will not include examples.
3. **Contrast**	The answer will emphasize the differences.
4. **Compare**	The answer will include both the similarities and the differences.
5. **Trace**	The answer will show the chronological progress of the idea.
6. **Debate** **Discuss** **Evaluate**	The answer will consider the question from various points of view. Evaluation means that you may express your opinion of it, pro and con.
7. **Justify**	Your answer will show the reasons for this action, presenting facts to support your position.
8. **Interpret**	Your answer will make clear what was meant and will show the underlying meaning.

Go to **P14**.

P16————————————————————

Write out the meaning of each letter in **SCORER** on the following page as applied to essay exams.

S = _____

C = _____

O = _____

R = _____

E = _____

R = _____

Check your answers in **P17**.

P17────────────────────

S	= **Schedule**	Schedule your time and your work. Organize your writing around a *core* of main ideas and *support* it by examples and facts.
C	= **Clue words**	Find the *clue words* that tell you what to write.
O	= **Omit the difficult questions**	*Answer the easy problems first;* postpone the difficult until later.
R	= **Read carefully**	*Read* the *instructions*. Read each *question* carefully and completely.
E	= **Estimate your answer**	Do *not* guess on long essay exams. Do not pad your answer. Be *direct* and to the point—estimate where you're going before you start writing.
R	= **Review your work**	Proofread the exam. Correct *grammar, punctuation, misspelling*. Is your name on the answer sheet? Were you *direct?* Did you use *examples?*

Good luck!

APPENDIX

Managing Time

"If I just had more time . . .!"

This common complaint about time is generally made because most people:

1. Haven't learned how to use time well
2. Don't really know what they want to do in life
3. Don't know how to go about getting what they do want
4. Procrastinate, or put off doing what they should
5. Spend too much time on things that aren't important to achieving personal goals

If one or all of the above reasons keep you from reaching your goals, we suggest you read Alan Lakein's *How to Get Control of Your Time and Your Life* (David McKay Publishers).

If you don't have time to read the book, you can read parts of it in the April, 1975 issue of *Reader's Digest*.

If you don't have time for that either, then take the time to do the following. **First**, in the spaces provided, list everything you need to do or must do tomorrow. Don't worry about the order of your list.

_____	_____
_____	_____
_____	_____
_____	_____
_____	_____

Now, look over your list and put the number 1 by the most important item, a 2 by the second most important, and so on. When finished, answer these questions.

1. Why is item number 1 the most important? _____

_____

2. Is it something you *can* do today? _____

_____

3. How much time will it take? _____

_____

4. Will you be able to do it, along with the other "have to's" on your

list? _____

5. How did you establish your priorities? _____

_____

6. Should you rearrange any of your priorities? _____ Explain.

_____

These are the sorts of questions you need to ask yourself as you plan a day's schedule. As a student, of course, you must be concerned with more than just one day. While making sure that you do use your time wisely each day, it is also necessary that you see beyond one day at a time in order to use each day well.

Look at Figure A. Have you ever completed a schedule like this for yourself? If you have trouble managing your time, you should. Look at the schedule carefully. Notice that at the top there are spaces to write in what must be done for the week, what previous assignments are still due, and what new assignments have been given to carry over into another week's schedule. This helps keep in mind what needs to be done in plotting out future weekly schedules.

Notice that each day of the week is planned around that day as well as what is coming up the next day or so. For instance, the Monday 7 p.m. study slot is reserved for studying psychology because the student's psych class meets the next morning. At 8 p.m., time is reserved for working on the English essay due Friday. And the 9 p.m. slot is reserved for studying history even though the history class doesn't meet until Wednesday. Why? Look at Tuesday's schedule. The student has a computer class that night. So in order to have Wednesday's history homework completed on time, it is necessary to do it on Monday.

The student doesn't have an easy schedule, carrying five classes and working 20 hours per week. But this student has **priorities**. There is little time for goofing off, and even though the schedule does not show 2 hours of homework for every hour in class (which is what college instructors expect), the student has a **flexible** schedule. Studying one subject can be shifted to another hour if need be. There is plenty of free time open on weekends if it becomes necessary to put in more hours of study. If it

STUDY SCHEDULE: WEEK OF __October 9-15__

This week's Must-do's:	Previous Assignments due:	New Assignments due:
① English essay due Friday ② Begin research for Psych term paper	① Revise book review for History by next week, Oct. 21.	① Finish Chap. 3 in study skills text by Oct. 28.

Time	MONDAY	TUESDAY	WEDNESDAY	THURSDAY	FRIDAY	SATURDAY	SUNDAY
7	←——— RISE AND SHINE! EAT ————→						
8	←—TRAVEL AND PARKING TIME————→ ←— LIBRARY - REVIEW/ READ/ PREPARE FOR CLASS——→					WORK	FREE
9	HISTORY	PSYCH	HISTORY	PSYCH	HISTORY		
10	Review Hist. notes / Review Eng. notes	↓	Review Hist notes / Review Eng. notes	↓	Review Hist. notes / Review Eng. notes		
11	ENGLISH	LUNCH	ENGLISH	LUNCH	ENGLISH		
12	Rev. Eng. notes LUNCH ↓	READING/ STUDY SKILLS Rev. notes	Rev. Eng. LUNCH ↓	READING/ STUDY SKILLS Rev. notes	Rev. Eng. LUNCH ↓	↓	
1	←— LEAVE SCHOOL FOR WORK ————→					LUNCH	
2	←———— WORK ————————→					LIBRARY RESEARCH	
3	←———— WORK ————————→					FREE	↓
4	←———— WORK ————————→						Read Lib Research
5	←———TRAVEL TIME HOME————→ ←————— EXERCISE ————→						Read Chap. 3 in study skills
6	←————DINNER———→ TRAVEL						DINNER
7	STUDY PSYCH	COMPUTER CLASS	STUDY PSYCH	STUDY HIST.	FREE		Study Hist.
8	Work on Eng. essay	↓	Finish Eng. essay	Read computer text			Study Eng.
9	Study Hist.	↓	Read computer text	Revise Eng. essay			FREE
10	FREE	TRAVEL FREE	FREE	FREE			↓
11	BED	BED	BED	BED			BED
	↓				↓	↓	↓

Figure A

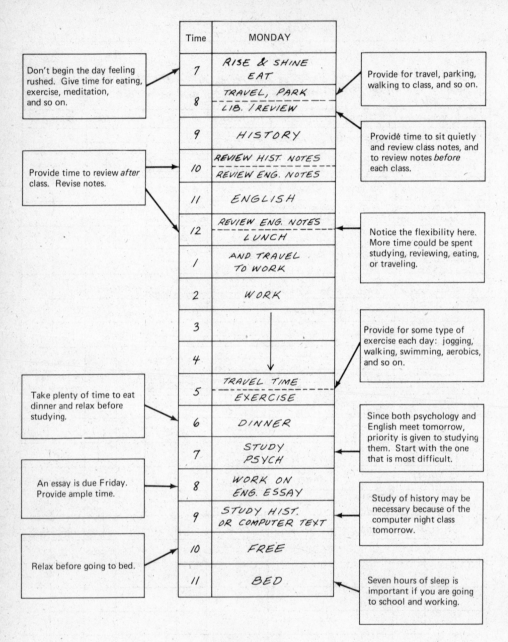

Time	MONDAY
7	RISE & SHINE EAT
8	TRAVEL, PARK LIB. / REVIEW
9	HISTORY
10	REVIEW HIST. NOTES REVIEW ENG. NOTES
11	ENGLISH
12	REVIEW ENG. NOTES LUNCH
1	AND TRAVEL TO WORK
2	WORK
3	
4	
5	TRAVEL TIME EXERCISE
6	DINNER
7	STUDY PSYCH
8	WORK ON ENG. ESSAY
9	STUDY HIST. OR COMPUTER TEXT
10	FREE
11	BED

Don't begin the day feeling rushed. Give time for eating, exercise, meditation, and so on.

Provide for travel, parking, walking to class, and so on.

Provide time to sit quietly and review class notes, and to review notes *before* each class.

Provide time to review *after* class. Revise notes.

Notice the flexibility here. More time could be spent studying, reviewing, eating, or traveling.

Provide for some type of exercise each day: jogging, walking, swimming, aerobics, and so on.

Take plenty of time to eat dinner and relax before studying.

Since both psychology and English meet tomorrow, priority is given to studying them. Start with the one that is most difficult.

An essay is due Friday. Provide ample time.

Study of history may be necessary because of the computer night class tomorrow.

Relax before going to bed.

Seven hours of sleep is important if you are going to school and working.

Figure B

turns out that not enough time is available for study and no time for relaxing, the student should consider either reducing the number of workhours, or reducing the number of classes. Again, this is where priorities must be considered. Don't try to carry more class units than you can reasonably handle.

Now look at Figure B, a day schedule. Read it carefully and study the marginal comments.

After you've looked carefully at Figures A and B, go to Figure C and make out a schedule of your own. Before you do, however, read the advice list below:

1. Schedules should be **flexible**. Time in class, job hours, travel time, etc. can't be changed. Be realistic and allow flexibility to switch times for certain events that can be changed.
2. Consider what is your **prime time**; that is, the time when you are freshest. Do your most difficult studying when you are at your best. Do the most interesting things last as a kind of reward for doing the most difficult work first.
3. Only you know if you need a half hour or 2 hours to read certain assignments. **Plan** your study time **realistically**. A 1-hour study block should really be 50 minutes with a 10-minute break, or 30 minutes with a 5-minute break.
4. Try to give yourself time before and after classes to **preview or review** class notes. When you schedule your classes, try to avoid taking them back to back. You need time in between.
5. Keep track of **long-term assignments**. Don't put off starting them until they are almost due.
6. **Relaxation** and **exercise** are very important to good studying. Don't sacrifice them for long hours of study. Allow for periodic breaks between study sessions. Research shows that more frequent short study periods are more productive than long ones.
7. If you stick to your schedule, plan a **reward** for yourself. We all need pats on the back.

If you're not used to making out a schedule and sticking to it, then it may be difficult for you to do it at first. But if you're not managing your time well now, it's worth a try for a few weeks. It helps you develop a discipline that no one else can teach you but yourself.

STUDY SCHEDULE: WEEK OF _____

This week's Must-do's:			Previous Assignments due:		New Assignments due:		

Time	MONDAY	TUESDAY	WEDNESDAY	THURSDAY	FRIDAY	SATURDAY	SUNDAY

Figure C

Glossary of College Terminology

Academic Senate An organization made up of faculty members of the college or university whose function is to either advise or govern administrative and instructional matters.

Academic titles Instruction is done by the following members of a faculty (listed in order of rank):

Professor The highest professional rank, usually a PhD.

Associate Professor The next highest rank, not necessarily a PhD.

Assistant Professor The lowest rank on the "professor" level.

Instructor A faculty member, usually not having tenure on the staff.

Lecturer A person who teaches at a college but does not have tenure or the rank of a regular faculty member.

Teaching Assistant (TA) Usually a graduate student who earns part of his or her college expenses by working for a full-time faculty member.

Student Teacher A student who is learning how to teach his or her major.

Advance placement Sometimes students are able to take college-level courses in high school and, if they pass the examination, they can obtain college credit for their work.

Alumna A woman graduate or former student.

Alumni The plural term for all graduates.

Alumnus A man graduate or former student.

A.A.   Refers to a 2-year college degree, the Associate of Arts Degree.

A.B.   Sometimes referred to as a B.A., a degree given to a student completing a 4-year program, the Bachelor of Arts Degree.

A.C.T.   An entrance test given to first-year students by many colleges and universities, the American College Testing program.

A.S.   Refers to a 2-year college degree, the Associate in Science Degree.

Auditing   Attending a course without receiving credit; usually exam requirements are waived.

B.A.   See A.B. above.

B.S.   A degree given to a student completing a 4-year program in the sciences, the Bachelor of Science Degree.

Bluebook   A standard examination booklet sold in campus bookstores and used for writing essay exams.

Class card   Usually an IBM card which is used to officially enroll a student in a particular course.

Credit by exam In some schools students who feel they have sufficient knowledge of a particular subject (either through independent study or work experience) can take an examination which, if they pass, gives them college credit, even though they have not actually taken the course. A national program offered at some colleges and universities is the College-Level Examination Program, also called CLEP.

Credit   The amount of work a student completes or attempts to complete is referred to as either credits, units, or hours. Each completed course is worth an established number of credits or units. To receive a degree, a specified number of credits or units is required.

Credit/No Credit See Pass/Fail system. Usually a grade of A, B, or C is recorded as a *credit* under this system. Any grade less than C is recorded as *no credit*.

Curriculum	A term referring to the various course offerings, or a particular group of courses required for a degree.
Deans	The head of a particular administrative college or university post, such as Dean of Students, Dean of Women, and so on.
Department	One of several units within a division. For example, the Social Science Division contains a History Department, an Economics Department, an Anthropology Department, and so on.
Division	A group of several departments. See **Department**.
Elective	A course a student may take which is not required by the institution.
E.O.P.S.	Extended Opportunities, Programs, and Services. This is a group of state and federally funded programs that supply assistance to low-income students, including tutorial help, counseling, and financial aid.
G.P.A.	Grade point average, or the overall grade equivalent based on the grades earned from all credits received.
Independent study	Earning credits for course work by working independently under the direction of a faculty member who is knowledgeable in the field of study undertaken.
Intramural sports	Sports contests within the college or university which do not involve competition with other schools.
Lower division	Refers to the freshman and sophomore years of study.
Master's Degree	Refers to a degree given a student for course work completed after receiving a B.A. degree; an M.A. ranks above a B.A. degree and is lower than a Ph.D. (M.A. = Master of Arts; M. E. = Master of Education; M.S. = Master of Science.)
Pass/Fail system	Rather than receiving grades for a course, it is sometimes possible to receive only a pass or fail mark on your record.

Petitions	A formal written request by a student who wishes to be exempted from a school policy, such as a petition for a change in major or a change in grade.
Ph.D.	Doctor of Philosophy degree; ranks above the Master's degree and entitles the person to be called "doctor."
Phi Beta Kappa	A national honorary society composed of students with extremely high grade-point averages.
Probation	When a student's grade-point average is below the school standard, that student is placed on probation and given a time period during which the student must raise his or her grades or be dismissed from school.
Quarter system	A system whereby the school year is divided into three parts plus a summer session; usually 10 weeks per quarter.
Registrar	The administrator in charge of all student records; the person to contact when you want a transcript of your grades.
S.A.T.	Scholastic Aptitude Test; generally administered to freshmen by the counseling staff to establish scores in reading, math, and vocabulary.
Semester system	A system that divides the school year in half; a semester usually lasts 15 or 16 weeks.
Seminar	A small group of students meeting with a professor for discussion of readings and research findings.
Student Health Services	Health services offered on campus to students attending.
Suspension	A period when a student is not permitted to attend school.
Transcript	A copy of a student's academic career which lists the courses taken, grades, grade-point average, and dates of completion; can be obtained from the registrar's office.

Undergraduate A student who has not completed the required work for a bachelor's degree.

Upper division The junior and senior years of study in a 4-year college.

Index